Adobe®
Photoshop CS5

Prentice Hall
is an imprint of

Harlow, England • London • New York • Boston • San Francisco • Toronto • Sydney • Singapore • Hong Kong
Tokyo • Seoul • Taipei • New Delhi • Cape Town • Madrid • Mexico City • Amsterdam • Munich • Paris • Milan

Pearson Education Limited
Edinburgh Gate
Harlow CM20 2JE
Tel: +44 (0)1279 623623
Fax: +44 (0)1279 431059
Website: www.pearsoned.co.uk

First published in Great Britain in 2011

Pearson Education is not responsible for the content of third party internet sites.

ISBN: 978-0-273-73682-0

British Library Cataloguing-in-Publication Data
A catalogue record for this book is available from the British Library

Library of Congress Cataloging-in-Publication Data
Benjamin, Louis.
  Adobe Photoshop CS5 in simple steps / Louis Benjamin.
     p. cm.
  ISBN 978-0-273-73682-0 (pbk.)
 1. Photography--Digital techniques. 2. Computer graphics. 3. Adobe Photoshop. I. Title
  TR267.5.A3B452 2010
  006.6'96--dc22   2010038324

Adobe product screen shots reprinted with permission from Adobe Systems Incorporated.

10 9 8 7 6 5 4 3 2 1
14 13 12 11 10

Typeset in 11/14 pt ITC Stone Sans by 3
Printed and bound in Great Britain by Scotprint Ltd, Haddington

Adobe®
Photoshop CS5

in Simple steps

Louis Benjamin

Use your computer with confidence

Get to grips with practical computing tasks with minimal time, fuss and bother.

In Simple Steps guides guarantee immediate results. They tell you everything you need to know on a specific application; from the most essential tasks to master, to every activity you'll want to accomplish, through to solving the most common problems you'll encounter.

Helpful features

To build your confidence and help you to get the most out of your computer, practical hints, tips and shortcuts feature on every page:

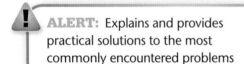

ALERT: Explains and provides practical solutions to the most commonly encountered problems

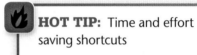

HOT TIP: Time and effort saving shortcuts

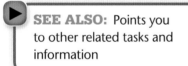

SEE ALSO: Points you to other related tasks and information

DID YOU KNOW?
Additional features to explore

WHAT DOES THIS MEAN?
Jargon and technical terms explained in plain English

Practical. Simple. Fast.

in Simple
steps

Dedication:

To Denise with zoo4ever.

Author acknowledgments:

Thanks especially to Zorana Gee, Vishal Khandpur and the CS5 team at Adobe. Per Gylfe at ICP has always given great support, and was one of the first to champion the CS4 edition of this book; I am grateful. Thanks again, Neil – you da man. Thanks also to Steve Temblett, Katy Robinson, Melanie Carter and the team at Pearson Education. It takes a village to publish a book.

My Photoshop students have been essential guides in writing this book. They constantly challenge me to find ways to demonstrate this sometimes-confounding tool in clear and concise terms and to make it relevant to their interests. I wrote this book with them in mind.

Finally, Mom and Dad gave me a great start in life, and give me inspiration and encouragement to this day.

Contents at a glance

Top 10 Photoshop CS5 Problems Solved

Contents

Top 10 Photoshop CS5 Tips

1 Getting started with Adobe Photoshop CS5

6 View, zoom and navigate

7 Paint and work with Brush tools

8 Work with selections

Top 10 Photoshop CS5 Problems Solved

Top 10 Photoshop CS5 tips

Tip 1: Use the Export panel

The Export panel in Adobe Bridge contains a set of Output modules that offer a streamlined way to batch export files to JPEGs. All of the Output modules work the way the basic Save to Hard Drive module does, with minor variations: you drop a set of files onto it to create a queue, specify a destination, set image options, and click a button to run the batch. The module then creates the JPEGs and places them in the specified location. Because the Output module can process Raw files, it opens the possibility of a workflow that goes from camera to web without touching Photoshop. You can also use Camera Raw to edit the Raw file, press Done and then drop it into the Export panel.

As this book is being written, there are also Output modules that can place files directly onto your Flickr, Facebook and Phtoshop.com accounts. Their destination tabs contain site-specific login and gallery options.

Click on the Export panel tab or choose Window, Export Panel from the menu bar to show it. Details on using the Save to Hard Drive module are below.

1 Drag files to the module.

2 Click the triangle to the left of the icon to show the files in the queue.

3 Hover the cursor over the items in the queue for the option to view the file in Bridge or delete it from the queue.

4 Click the X on the Save to Hard Drive module to cancel the entire queue.

5 Click the arrow or double-click the module to edit the destination and image options.

6 In the Destination tab: set the location and specify how the new files should be named.

7 In the Image Options tab: set the file size, resample method, image quality and metadata to be applied.

8 Click Export to run the batch.

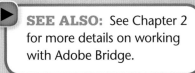

SEE ALSO: See Chapter 2 for more details on working with Adobe Bridge.

Tip 2: Create a web gallery with the Output module

You can select several files in Bridge and build a web gallery in a fashion similar to creating a slideshow, just with more info to specify. Use the triangles on the left edge of each section of the dialogue to expand and collapse them.

The Web Gallery feature comes with a number of pre-defined templates, including three styles from Airtight. In this example, we'll be working with the extremely popular SimpleViewer template.

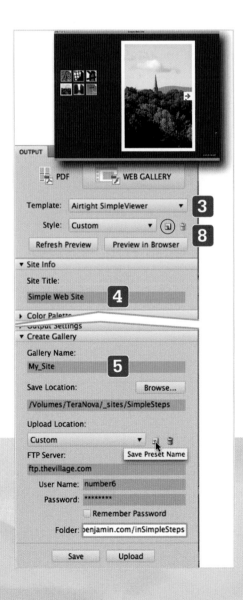

1 Select Output from the Workspace Switcher or click on the Output icon in the header section.

2 Click the Web Gallery button in the Output panel.

3 Choose Airtight SimpleViewer from the Template menu.

4 In the Site Info section, enter the Site Title.

5 Fill in the Create Gallery section. You can type in a path or click Browse to point to a location on your hard disk to save your gallery. You don't have to enter FTP data if you plan to use a standalone FTP tool.

6 If you don't want people to Ctrl-click/right-click on your web gallery and download your images, be sure that Allow right-click to open photos is not ticked under Output Settings.

7 Adjust other attributes under Color Palette, Appearance and Image Info as you like.

8 Optional: click the Save Style icon to add your settings to the Style menu.

9 Click Preview in Browser to see what your gallery looks like with up to 10 images.

10 Click Save to write a copy of your gallery to the hard drive and click Upload to send your gallery directly to the web server.

 HOT TIP: If you're using captions with your image, you can adjust caption data quickly with the File Info dialogue.

 SEE ALSO: See Chapter 2 for more details on working with Adobe Bridge.

Tip 3: Make a PDF with the Output module

In a fashion similar to creating websites and slideshows, Bridge can combine a selection of images into a PDF file. It can even be set so that upon opening, the PDF expands to full screen mode, and plays the images as a slideshow. Use the triangles on the left edge of each section of the dialogue to expand and collapse them.

1 Select Output from the Workspace Switcher or click on the Output icon in the header section.

2 Click the PDF icon.

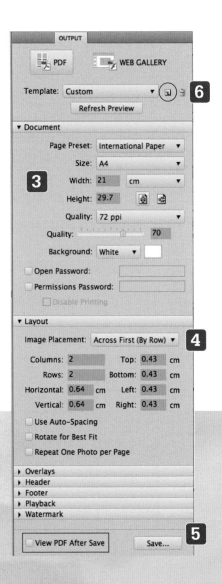

3 In the Document section, specify the paper size, orientation, image quality, background colour and optional passwords.

4 Use the controls in the Layout section of the panel to specify how images will be arranged.

5 Optional:

- If you want to review the PDF as soon as you save it, make sure that the box marked View PDF After Save is checked.
- Add the filename and page numbering in the Overlays section.
- Add headers and footers.
- Set automatic playback options including Full Screen Mode and transitions.
- Add a watermark.

6 Optional: click the Save Template icon to add the settings to the Template menu.

7 Click Refresh Preview to see what the first page will look like. The preview appears in a tab with the Preview panel.

8 Click Save … and use the controls in the Save As dialogue to name your PDF and specify where it will be saved.

9 Click Save.

Tip 4: Use noise reduction

Digital noise tends to be a problem when shooting at high ISO, and it is more pronounced on cameras with smaller sensor chips (e.g. APS or DX). It comes in two forms. Colour noise occurs as bright, coloured dots that appear in a random pattern, particularly in the shadows. Luminance noise is when the pixels are too light or too dark compared to the surrounding pixels. Noise becomes even more of a problem as you try to lighten dark images.

The noise reduction feature in Camera Raw works well, and is simple to use. Adobe rewrote the noise reduction feature for Camera Raw 6/Photoshop CS5. The new version is remarkably better at preserving colour and detail.

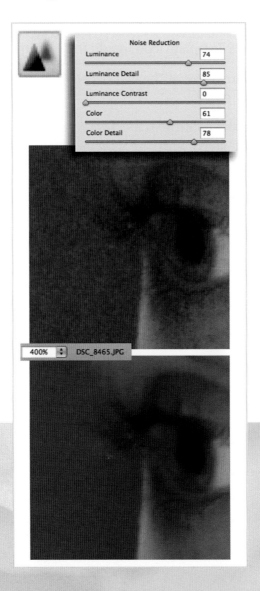

1 Click on the Detail icon to bring up the sharpening and noise reduction controls.

2 Zoom in to at least 100% to see the effects of these controls clearly.

3 Use the Luminance slider to even out luminance noise.

4 The Luminance Detail and Luminance Contrast controls become available when you move the Luminance slider above zero. Use them to refine the image further.

5 Use the Color and Color Detail sliders to remove colour noise.

ALERT: For best results, be sure to use the current (2010) process. If you see an exclamation mark in the lower right corner of the image area, click it to update the process.

HOT TIP: Even though there are sharpening controls in Camera Raw, sharpening is usually done in Photoshop at the end of the editing process. The sharpening controls are available under this tab for two reasons – sometimes, a bit of preview sharpening can help during the adjustment process. Second, there are some workflows that are Camera Raw – only.

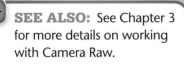

SEE ALSO: See Chapter 3 for more details on working with Camera Raw.

Tip 5: Soften wrinkles

The aesthetics of retouching varies a lot and is a matter of personal taste. Some people insist on having all of their wrinkles removed, but that generally produces a very unnatural look. An alternative is to use the Clone Stamp to create a smoothed-out version of someone's skin, and then fade the retouching a bit to restore some of the original texture beneath. The result is a more believable look. In this example, we'll copy the area we want to repair into its own layer so that we can use the Clone Stamp with a blending mode.

1 Make a loose selection around the area that you want to soften and use Command + J to copy the selection to a new layer.

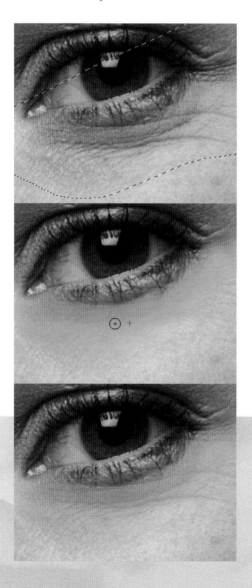

2 To knock down the shadows that make up the lines, use a small Clone Stamp (not much larger than the lines themselves) in Lighten mode. A round brush with a hardness of zero will work well. Set Sample to Current & Below. Set Flow and Opacity to the range of 30–40% to build slowly.

3 Brush over the dark lines. You can use Aligned, but be sure to Option/Alt – click from time to time to change the sampling location. Keep the source very close to the brush and copy from slightly lighter skin. The lines will diminish but not vanish completely.

4 To burnish the area, set the Clone Stamp to normal mode, keeping the Flow and Opacity low. Increase the brush size slightly and pass back and forth over the same areas with different sources each time. Be careful not to shift the tone too much. The texture of the area will become increasingly smooth.

5 When the retouch layer is sufficiently smoothed out, reduce its Opacity until some of the lines return in a subdued way. In this example, the layer was faded to 65%.

> **SEE ALSO:** See Chapter 10 for details on retouching and Chapter 8 for details on making selections.

Tip 6: Adjust colour with auto curves

The Auto button in the curves dialogue has a number of preset routines for improving the appearance of an image. It's no panacea, but the options are useful. To determine which adjustment works best for your image, it's best to step through the various options. Sometimes the resulting curve improves colour but degrades the tone. To address this, you can change the blending mode of the curve to Color.

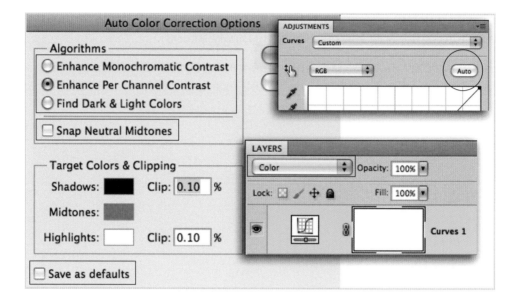

1 Add a Curves adjustment layer.

2 Hold down the Option/Alt key on your keyboard and click the Auto button in the Adjustments panel. The Auto Color Correction Options dialogue will appear.

3 Leave the box next to Snap Neutral Midtones unchecked.

4 Click on the circle next to each of the three options in the Algorithms section, noting which looks better.

5 Check the box next to Snap Neutral Midtones.

6 Click on the circle next to each of the three options in the Algorithms section, noting which looks better.

7 Compare the best of the results with Snap Neutral Midtones checked to those with Snap Neutral Midtones unchecked to determine the best course of auto correction.

8 Optional: tick Save as defaults to apply that method whenever you click the Auto button.

9 Click the OK button.

10 Optional: change the blending mode of the Curves layer to Color.

SEE ALSO: See Chapter 11 for more on adjusting colour and tone.

Tip 7: Black and white and colour in the same image

If you use a Black & White adjustment layer to convert your colour image, you can use its built-in layer mask to create a popular effect: simply black out the parts of the mask where you want the colour to show through. Making the effect work well depends upon the precision of your painting or selection, and you have a number of potential selection tools at your disposal. Beyond the usual effect, be sure to try different black and white conversions, blending modes and opacities.

1. Create a selection and then add the Black & White layer.

2. Add a Black & White layer (white mask) and then paint black into the mask by hand.

3. Add a Black & White layer (white mask), create a selection, and use Edit, Fill to black out parts of the mask.

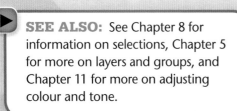

SEE ALSO: See Chapter 8 for information on selections, Chapter 5 for more on layers and groups, and Chapter 11 for more on adjusting colour and tone.

Tip 8: Use HDR toning

HDR Toning creates the look of High Dynamic Range (HDR) images without the elaborate multi-exposure process needed to create true HDR images. The tool performs a destructive edit on flattened images, so be sure to save a layered master copy of your image before you apply the adjustment.

1 Select Image, Adjustments, HDR Toning from the menu bar.

2 Use a preset or select a toning method.

3 Adjust relevant controls (the Equalize Histogram and Highlight Compression methods do not have controls).

4 Toggle the preview to evaluate.

5 Optional: save a preset via the icon next to the Preset menu.

6 Click OK.

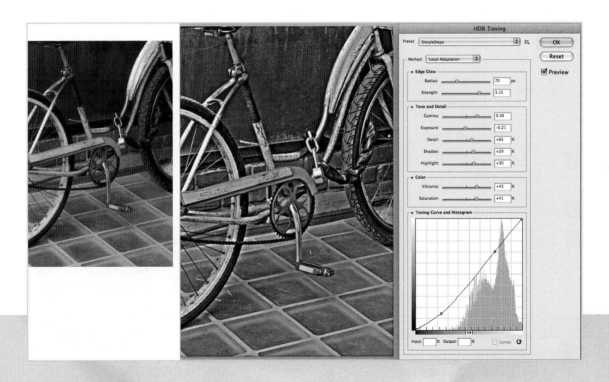

Tip 9: Use the File Info dialogue and enter your copyright notice

The File info dialogue is available in both Bridge and Photoshop. It is just one way of entering metadata, especially your name and copyright notice, into your images.

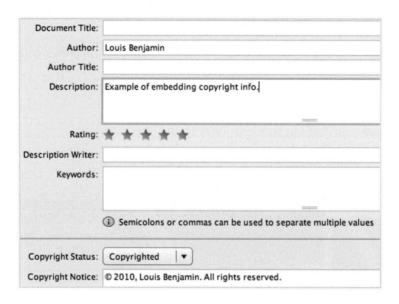

1 Use Command/Ctrl + I to open the File info dialogue, or choose File Info ... either from the Refine menu in the header area of Bridge, or from the File menu.

2 Click on the Description tab.

3 Enter Author, Description and Keywords (separated by semicolons or commas) as needed.

ALERT: Technically, the proper way to write a copyright notice is either to spell out the word or to use the symbol, which is a c inside a circle. (c) is not actually recognised as a proper copyright symbol.

4 Select Copyrighted from the Copyright Status menu.

5 Enter your copyright notice, beginning with the copyright symbol: Option + g on the Mac, Alt + 0169 on Windows.

6 Click OK.

 HOT TIP: If you tag or keyword your images in Bridge, that information will also appear when you open them in Photoshop. This info is also embedded into any JPEG or TIFF files you export, making the images identifiable by search engines, including Apple's Spotlight.

 DID YOU KNOW?

These are only some of the items you can embed in your image through the File Info dialogue. The Description, IPTC and IPTC Extension tabs are just three pages of the dialogue that have enterable fields. This is a tool worth getting familiar with.

 SEE ALSO: See Chapter 2 for more on adding metadata and managing your files with Adobe Bridge.

Tip 10: Get files from your camera

Adobe Bridge has a built-in tool called Adobe Photo Downloader, which allows you to import files from your camera's media card on to your computer's hard disk. It can help you organise those files and apply metadata as it does so.

Of course, there are several ways to get files into your computer from your camera. If you are already comfortable using another way, it is not imperative that you stop doing that and use Photo Downloader instead. However, it is a useful tool with some features that can make simple work of the process.

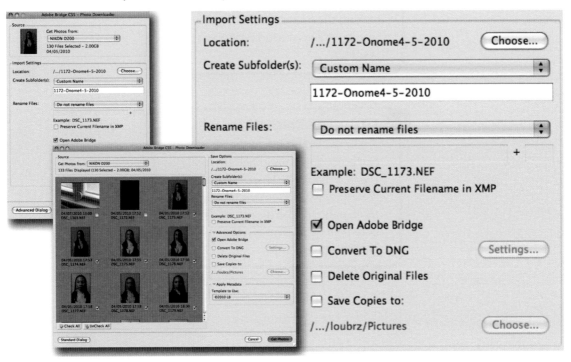

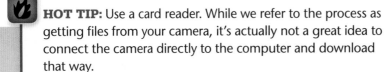

HOT TIP: Use a card reader. While we refer to the process as getting files from your camera, it's actually not a great idea to connect the camera directly to the computer and download that way.

A better approach is to get a memory card reader that matches your camera's format (usually Compact Flash or SD, though there are others). You plug the card into the reader, and the reader into your computer. Downloading that way will go faster and won't drain your camera's batteries.

1 Select File, Get Photos from Camera ... from the menu bar.

2 Optional: click the Advanced Dialogue button for more features.

3 Click Choose ... to select a parent folder to hold your files.

4 Set options, such as creating and naming subfolders as needed.

5 If you are using the Advanced dialogue, tick the photos you want to download (recommend all), and optionally select a metadata template (e.g. your copyright) to apply.

6 Click Get Photos.

? DID YOU KNOW?
You can use the Mac Finder or Windows to download, too. Create a new folder, mount your media card and then drag the contents of the media card to the folder.

▶ **SEE ALSO:** The Set key preferences section of Chapter 2 discusses the option to Launch Photo Downloader automatically whenever you plug in a media card.

1 Getting started with Adobe Photoshop CS5

Introduction

In this chapter, we'll look at some key elements of the Adobe Photoshop interface and cover some initial setup. Photoshop is a big application, designed to suit a number of different types of users, including photographers, graphic designers, pre-press specialists, and others. We're going to optimise it for photographic work.

It is worth noting immediately that even though we talk in terms of 'editing in Photoshop', the process often entails a workflow that may involve visiting two related environments — Adobe Bridge and Adobe Camera Raw. This book is arranged to reflect the ways in which you might typically work with photographic images, and discusses Photoshop, Bridge and Camera Raw in the sequence that you're likely to use them in that workflow.

As you explore and learn about Photoshop, you will quickly discover that there are lots of ways to do the same thing, and you will also find out about features and techniques not covered in this book. Most of the more advanced Photoshop techniques that you will encounter are founded on the basics covered here. The aim is to provide you with a solid foundation of best practices for working with Photoshop. So, let's begin ...

Reset all preferences to the default settings

Because Photoshop and Bridge are highly configurable, it can be very confusing to start trying to use these applications in a shared setting where the last person has rearranged the workspace and set preferences to work in a completely different manner from that which you are accustomed to. It could also be that you've been tinkering with Photoshop and changed a preference that you don't know how to undo, or in rare situations, your preferences file might have been damaged and Photoshop is behaving strangely. Resetting all of your preferences in one shot will get you back to a familiar configuration. From there, you can recustomise the settings the way you like.

To reset all of your preferences for Photoshop or Bridge back to the default settings, do the following:

1 Quit the application.

2 Hold down Shift + Option/Alt + Command/Ctrl and restart the application.

3 Continue holding the keys until you see a dialogue box asking what you'd like to do.

4 For Photoshop, click Yes.

5 For Bridge, tick the box marked Reset Preferences. You also have the option of purging the thumbnail cache. (If in doubt, don't purge.) Then click OK.

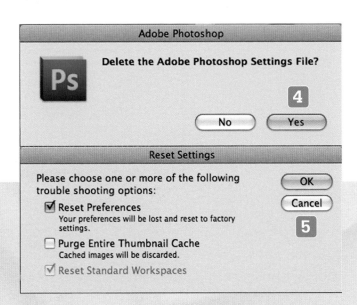

Set key preferences in Photoshop

There are actually three separate sets of configurations that could be called preferences in Photoshop. One set lives under the Photoshop menu (the Edit menu on Windows), while the preferences for colour management can be found under the Edit menu, and you can manage the arrangement of your panels through the Workspace menu.

1 Select Photoshop, Preferences, General … (Edit, Preferences, General … on Windows) from the menu bar to open that preference page. (Shortcut: Command/Ctrl + K.)

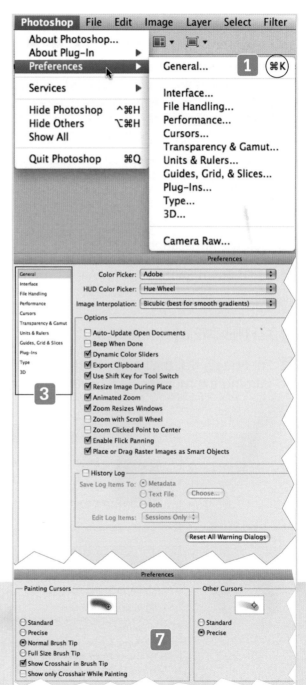

2 Tick the options that you prefer to use. Some recommended settings:

- HUD Colour Picker: Hue Wheel
- Image Interpolation: Bicubic
- Tick the box next to Resize Image During Place
- Tick the box next to Place or Drag Master Images as Smart Objects

3 Click the word Performance in the box at the left edge of the dialogue to switch between preference pages.

4 In the History and Cache section of the Performance page, increase the number of History States to approximately 50.

5 In the GPU settings section of the Performance page, the preference labelled Enable OpenGL Drawing should be ticked. If you are not able to tick it, your computer does not support the feature. (See the alert for details.)

6 Click the word Cursors in the box at the left to switch to the Cursors page.

7 In the Painting Cursors section, be sure that Normal Brush Tip is selected and that Show Crosshair in Brush Tip is ticked. Check to see that Precise is selected in the Other Cursors section.

8 Click OK to save changes to all pages, or Cancel to cancel all pages.

HOT TIP: If you don't know what a particular preference does, hold the mouse pointer still over the option. Depending on the preferences page, either a tool tip will appear or you'll see a description in the box at the bottom of the dialogue.

ALERT: OpenGL is a feature that is built into more advanced graphics cards from NVIDEA and ATI. While one of these cards is likely to be built into most computers sold in the last three years or so, you won't be able to use some features in Photoshop if your computer's graphics card doesn't support OpenGL drawing.

Set and save colour settings

An important aspect of working with photographs is maintaining accurate colour. By setting a colour space and establishing policies on how to handle conflicting or missing colour information, you can be assured of accurate colour whether you are printing an image or preparing to post it on the Internet.

1 From the Edit menu, choose Color Settings ... (Shortcut: Shift + Command/Ctrl + K).

2 From the Settings menu at the top of the dialogue box, choose Europe Prepress 3.

3 In the Working Spaces section, locate the Gray menu and change it from Dot Gain 15% to Gray Gamma 2.2. (This will change options in the menus below, and the Settings menu will now say Custom.)

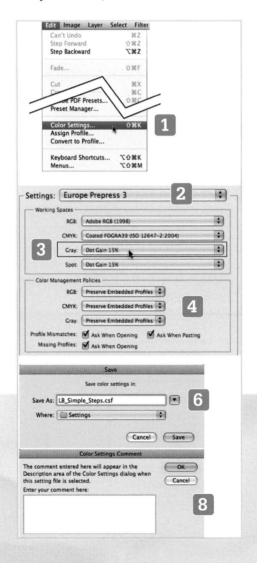

4 Leave the colour management policies set to preserve the embedded profiles and to ask when there are profile mismatches or missing profiles.

5 Click Save.

6 In the Save As box, enter a meaningful name such as General Photo. If you are using a copy of Photoshop that is on a shared computer, it is a good idea to include your initials in the name of the preference set.

7 Click Save.

8 When the Color Settings Comment box appears, you must click OK to finish saving the settings. Do not click the Cancel button.

9 Click OK to exit the Color Settings Dialogue.

ALERT: When the Color Settings Comment box appears, do not click the Cancel button, or your settings will not be saved. You don't have to enter a comment.

Set preferences for Adobe Camera Raw

Camera Raw is a plug-in, meaning there is no separate application to launch. It is available as an on-demand resource inside both Photoshop and Bridge. You can adjust your Camera Raw preferences from either Photoshop or Bridge. Advanced users may have specific reasons to diverge from the settings recommended below, but these general-purpose settings will suit a wide range of uses.

1 In Photoshop: Select Photoshop, Preferences, Camera Raw ... (Windows: Edit, Preferences, Camera Raw ...).

2 In Bridge: Select Adobe Bridge CS5, Camera Raw Preferences ... (Windows: Edit, Camera Raw Preferences ...).

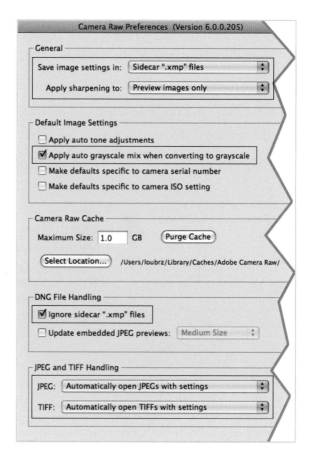

HOT TIP: Every digital camera has a different raw format, and that means that each time a manufacturer releases a new camera, Adobe has to release an update to Camera Raw that can read the new raw format. Windows and Mac OS also have to update some of their resources. As a result, there is often a slight lag between the time new cameras start shipping and when you can use their raw files with Photoshop.

ALERT: Camera Raw can't process layered TIFF files. Opening JPEG or TIFF files with Camera Raw doesn't turn them into raw files. You have the benefit of doing all of your initial edits in the same interface, but some features and capabilities of raw files are not available in those file formats.

3 In the General section of the dialogue, set Save image settings into Sidecar '.xmp' files and set Apply sharpening to Preview images only.

4 In the Default Image Settings section, it's best to only tick the box marked Apply auto grayscale mix when converting to grayscale.

5 If you choose to work with the DNG format, be sure to tick the option Ignore sidecar '.xmp' files. That's what tells Camera Raw to store the adjustments in the DNG file.

6 Set the JPEG and TIFF menus to Automatically open [file type]s with settings.

7 Click OK.

WHAT DOES THIS MEAN?

XMP, DNG, Camera Raw Database: unlike editing in Photoshop, when Camera Raw processes an image file, it essentially builds a recipe for how to transform the image into the edited version that you see in the preview and then passes a copy of the image with those edits applied over to Photoshop. It keeps the original file intact, and stores the recipe separately. This protects the original information from being degraded, and that is what is meant by non-destructive editing. Each time you reopen and adjust the raw file, the recipe data are updated. There are three ways that this recipe data can be stored. That's what XMP, etc. are all about.

XMP or 'sidecar' files: separate files that sit alongside the original raw file. The name of the file matches that of the raw file, except that it has an extension of .xmp instead of .nef, .cr2, etc. (e.g. DSC_1234.nef and DSC_1234.xmp). When you open a raw file in Camera Raw, it looks for a matching XMP file. If it finds one, it uses the enclosed recipe. If you delete the XMP, rename either the raw or XMP file so they no longer match, or move the raw file on to a new disc without the companion XMP, Camera Raw will treat the raw file as if it had never been edited. The implication is that when you copy or move raw files, you should make it a point to copy or move the matching XMP files along with them.

DNG (Adobe Digital Negative) files: these combine the original raw file and the sidecar file along with other metadata into a single document – when you copy or move a DNG file, everything goes along with it. This means there are no XMP files to keep track of. The DNG format is a published standard, which offers some archival benefits worth reading about. See www.adobe.com/products/dng/ for more information. The downside is that converting your raw files to DNG adds more steps to your workflow, and can add significant processing time.

The Camera Raw database: a special file that is stored in a single central location on your computer. It captures internal data from the raw files that you edit to keep track of them, so even if you rename a file, Camera Raw will find and apply the appropriate edits. When you use the database option there are normally no XMP files, but you can export XMPs when you need them.

What about JPEG and TIFF files? When you edit these files in Camera Raw, a copy of the original image is stored inside the file along with the recipe for rendering the adjustments.

Work with the Tools panel, Options bar and other panels

Selecting, painting, cropping, retouching and other activities are applied through tools that you activate via the Tools panel. In fact, a very large part of the Photoshop interface is operated through panels, which can be arranged or hidden according to your needs. By default, these panels are situated around the workspace with the Tools panel on the left, the Options bar along the top, and the Dock on the right. The contents of the Dock will be discussed in greater detail later in this chapter and beyond.

The Window menu lets you open or close any of the Photoshop panels. When a panel is open, a tick appears by its name in the menu. When you can't find a panel that you

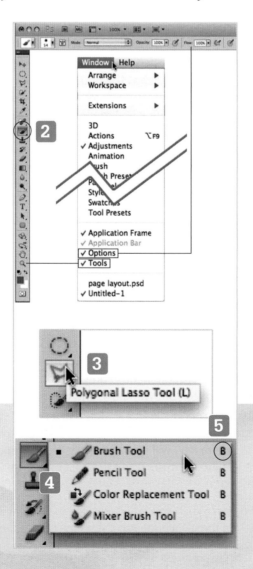

need, you can use the Window menu to reveal it. If there is a tick in the menu but you can't see the panel that you're looking for, just select it twice from the menu – once to close it and once to reopen it.

The list below describes various ways of selecting tools to work with.

1 To activate a tool, click on its icon in the Tools panel.

2 When you activate a tool, its button takes on a 3-D appearance and the Options bar updates to show relevant controls.

3 Hold the mouse pointer still over a button in the Tools panel to see a tool tip describing it.

4 A triangle in the lower right corner of a tool button indicates that a fly-out menu is available. Hold the mouse button down on any of these buttons to select among families of nested tools.

5 You can tap the letter key shortcut shown in the tool tip or fly-out menu to activate a tool (e.g. tap B to select the Brush tool).

6 Hold the shift key down and tap the shortcut key to cycle through the tools nested within the button (e.g. Shift + L to switch between the Lasso, Polygonal Lasso, and Magnetic Lasso tools).

 HOT TIP: If your Tools panel, Options bar and Dock all disappear at the same time, try hitting the tab key. If only one of these has disappeared, you probably closed it inadvertently. You can reset the entire workspace or you can reopen the missing panel through the Window menu. More on workspaces later in this chapter.

Use the Dock – panel and icon displays

The Dock is a flexible tool for organising panels in Photoshop. By default, it has two columns of panels: a wide column displaying panels with their active interfaces, and a narrow column of panels that are minimised to small icons. Tabs allow groups of panels to share the same space in a wide column.

The Dock itself can be torn away and floated free of the rest of the Photoshop interface. Floating windows can be reattached to one of several anchor points around the edges of the Photoshop environment.

Below are just a few examples of ways to configure and navigate with the Dock.

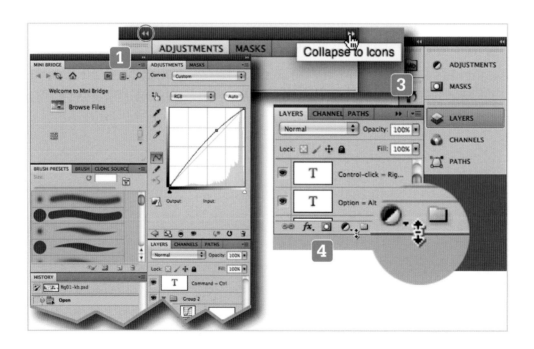

? DID YOU KNOW?

There are too many features and subtle ways in which panels and the Dock work to document them all here. Spend a bit of time experimenting – it will save you time in the long run.

1. To expand an icon column, click the double triangles at the right edge of the dark band at the top of the column.

2. Click the double triangles to collapse wide columns to icons, too.

3. Click an icon button to open its panel interface.

4. Drag the bottom and left edges of a panel to resize it.

5. Click an icon button again to hide the panel.

 HOT TIP: The Dock is actually just one of several areas in Photoshop where you can anchor panels. This will be discussed in greater detail later in this chapter.

Use the Dock – window shade, tabs, resize columns

Photoshop can stack several panels into a much smaller space by using tab groups. The window shade effect decreases that space further by shrinking the panel display and showing only a narrow band of tabs. When you window shade a set of tabs, other panels in the Dock, such as the Layers panel, can expand.

1 Double-click on a tab or in the blank area to the right of the tabs to shrink or expand tab groups using the window shade effect.

2 Click on a tab to activate that panel. Window shaded panels will expand automatically.

3 Drag tabs to the right or left to reorder a tab group.

4 Drag the vertical line at the left edge of a column in the Dock to make it wider or narrower.

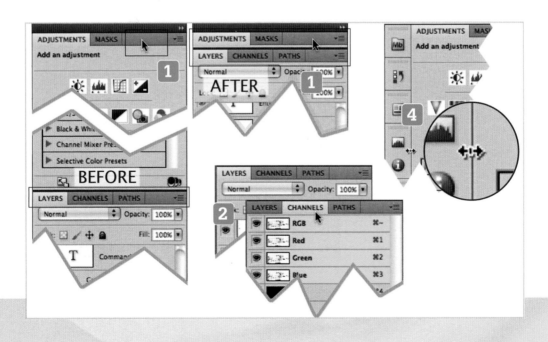

 HOT TIP: You can drag all of the panels in a tab group together by dragging the grey area shown in item 1 above. Later in this chapter, we'll look at reorganising panels.

Use the Dock – float a panel, add a column

Even though it can be tidy to keep your panels confined to the Dock, there may be times when you want that panel a lot closer to the place where you're working. That way, you're not dragging the mouse back and forth over miles of screen. You can tear a panel off the Dock and float it inches from where you're working intensively with that brush. There may be times, as well, where two columns of panels aren't enough. You can easily create more columns, simply by dragging panels.

1 To tear a panel off the dock, just drag it away and it will release.

2 If the panel is minimised to an icon, you can click the icon to show or hide its panel; or you can click the double triangles in the upper right corner to expand the panel.

3 To close a floating panel, click the circle in the upper left corner.

4 To add a column to the dock, drag a panel to the left edge of an existing column and release the mouse button when a vertical blue line appears.

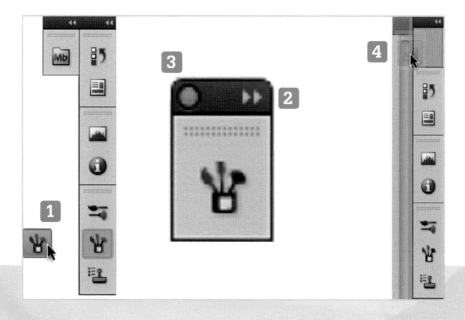

Dock panels and close tabs with the panel menu

Docking panels is as easy as detaching them, but it helps to know how to control the docking, otherwise you can end up with some out-of-control arrangements. Once you have separated a panel or a tab group from its original location, do one of the following:

1 Drag your panel(s) to a tab group and place the tip of the mouse pointer on one of the tabs. When a blue rectangle appears around the entire set, release the mouse button. Your panel(s) will be added to the set.

2 While dragging, place the tip of the mouse pointer on the line between two sets of panels. When a horizontal blue line appears, release the mouse button. The panels above and below will resize and your panel(s) will appear between them.

3 Drag to the bottom of a button in an icon column. Release the mouse button when a horizontal blue line appears.

A menu icon appears at the upper right corner of every panel and tab group. It contains options for the active panel, as well as for the entire tab group.

4 To close the current tab, choose Close from the menu.

5 To close the entire group, choose Close Tab Group from the menu.

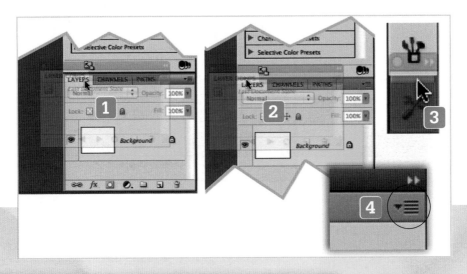

 HOT TIP: If you close a panel or group that you didn't mean to, remember that you can always retrieve your panels with the Window menu. You can also reset the workspace.

Anchor Mini Bridge to the bottom of your work area

Mini Bridge is a handy tool for quickly selecting an image to work on without switching out of Photoshop. By default, it appears as an icon button in the upper left corner of the Dock. A more efficient configuration for it is along the bottom of the work area. You can window shade it when it's not needed. That way, you can take advantage of its more efficient filmstrip layout and it only takes up room when it's needed.

To anchor Mini Bridge at the bottom of your work area, follow the steps below. (Don't be concerned if your screen does not exactly match this – we're experimenting with configuring the workspace, remember?)

1 Drag Mini Bridge to the bottom of the Photoshop work area.

2 When a blue horizontal line appears, release the mouse button.

3 Double click on the Mini Bridge tab to window shade it.

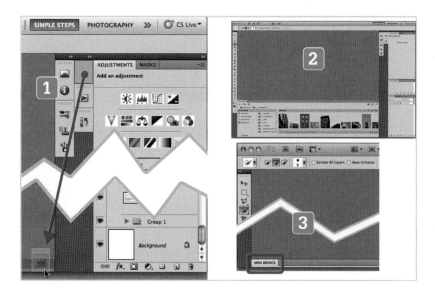

HOT TIP: Once Mini Bridge is at the bottom of your work area, you can drag the top edge of the panel up or down to resize it.

SEE ALSO: As the name suggests, Mini Bridge is not a replacement for Bridge, but we'll discuss the two applications in greater detail in the next chapter.

Save a custom workspace

You can create task-specific arrangements of panels and save them to the Workspace Switcher. For example, you can have one workspace that's optimal for retouching and a different one for annotation. This feature is particularly useful in situations such as schools, where a number of people are sharing a computer. Each user can configure Photoshop's interface as they need it, and save that workspace with their name on it. Setting up small, efficient workspaces can also be helpful if you're working with a small screen.

1 Select New Workspace ... from the menu in the Workspace Switcher or select Window, Workspace, New Workspace ... from the menu bar. The New Workspace dialogue will appear.

2 Enter the name of your choosing (e.g. Basic Photo).

3 Leave Keyboard Shortcuts and Menus unticked, since we have not altered any of those settings.

4 Click the Save button.

5 Note that the name of your saved workspace now appears in the Workspace Switcher.

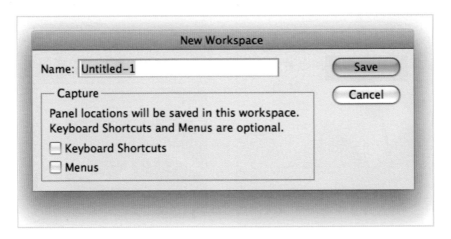

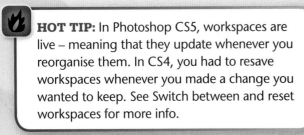

HOT TIP: In Photoshop CS5, workspaces are live – meaning that they update whenever you reorganise them. In CS4, you had to resave workspaces whenever you made a change you wanted to keep. See Switch between and reset workspaces for more info.

Switch between and reset workspaces

In Photoshop CS5, switching between workspaces is much faster than in previous versions, and the workspaces are live. This means that you can activate a workspace, move panels around, then switch to another workspace, and when you return, Photoshop will restore the most recent arrangement of the former workspace.

If you don't like a change that you made to the arrangement of a workspace, you can reset the workspace to restore the arrangement it had when it was originally saved. This includes the standard workspaces that come with Photoshop.

1 To switch between workspaces, do any of the following:

- Click one of the buttons on the Workspace Switcher.
- Select an item from the Workspace Switcher menu.
- Select the workspace from the Window, Workspace menu.

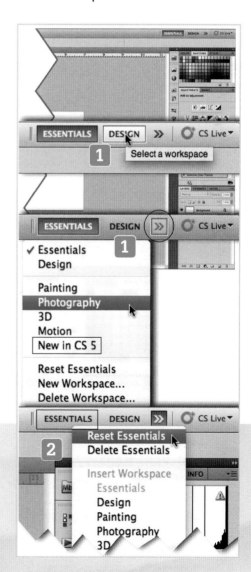

2 To reset a workspace, do any of the following:

- Ctrl-click/right-click on its button in the Workspace Switcher and choose Reset [workspace name] from the menu.

- Choose Reset [workspace name] from the Workspace Switcher menu.

- Select Window, Workspace, Reset [workspace name] from the menu bar.

Delete a workspace

You can't delete the active workspace, so if the workspace you want to get rid of is active, switch to another workspace, and then delete the workspace using one of the following two methods:

1 If the workspace is in one of the visible buttons, Ctrl-click/right-click on the workspace button and choose Delete [workspace name] from the menu.

2 Click Yes to confirm or No to cancel.

3 Or, you can choose Window, Workspace, Delete Workspace ... from the menu bar. The Delete Workspace dialogue will appear.

4 Select the workspace you want to delete from the menu.

5 Click Delete.

6 Click Yes to confirm or No to cancel.

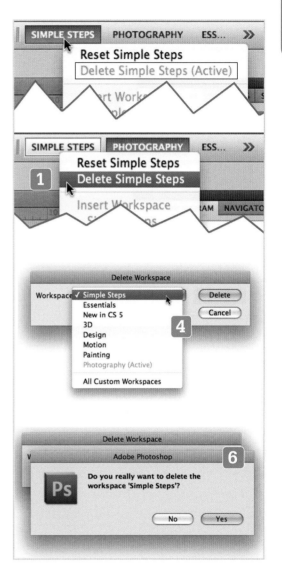

 HOT TIP: If you accidentally delete one of the workspaces that were installed with Photoshop, choose Photoshop, Preferences, Interface ... (Windows: Edit, Preference, Interface ...) and click Restore Default Workspaces.

2 Browse, show, manage and batch process images with Adobe Bridge

Introduction

Perhaps surprisingly, we begin this chapter about Adobe Bridge, working in Photoshop. We're going to look at how Photoshop and Bridge collaborate, both in terms of switching between the two applications, and through Mini Bridge.

Mini Bridge is a light version of Adobe Bridge in the form of a configurable Photoshop panel. This new feature brings built-in browsing back to Photoshop with a twist — Bridge runs in the background, providing resources to Mini Bridge so that it doesn't tax Photoshop the way the old file browser did.

Mini Bridge uses Bridge to create thumbnails, keep files synchronised, and perform other tasks. When you need the full features of Bridge, Mini Bridge makes it easy to take your current selection of images with you as you switch to and from Bridge.

Browsing for files, and especially when combining multiple files into a single Photoshop document, is more streamlined because of Mini Bridge. However, Mini Bridge is focused on browsing. The full Bridge application can present slideshows, make web galleries and export PDF files easily.

Use Mini Bridge

With Mini Bridge, you can browse, search, select and open files from within Photoshop. A button to launch Mini Bridge is conveniently located in the top left area of the Photoshop window (see item 8). Click the Mb button to show Mini Bridge, and click the Browse Files icon as needed. If Bridge is not running, there will be a slight delay while it starts up. Note: in this example, Mini Bridge has been moved from its default location and docked to the bottom of the work area.

1 Double-click the Mini Bridge tab to collapse the panel or click on the tab to expand with the window shade effect.

2 Browse other locations by using the navigation arrows, the navigation menu and the home icon, or by clicking items in the Path Bar.

3 Use the Navigation Pod to browse among favourites, recent files and folders, and collections.

4 Move the slider to adjust the size of thumbnails, or click on the icons at either end.

5 Use the View menu at the lower right corner of the Content area to change its layout.

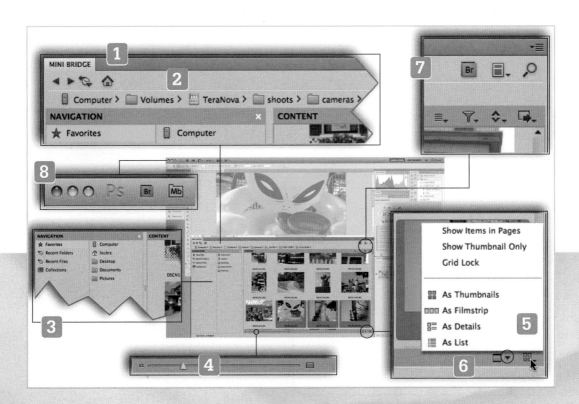

6 Click the triangle to the left of the View icon to set Slideshow options and choose between Slideshow, Review mode and two different Preview modes.

7 Click the Br button in the Mini Bridge panel to go to Bridge with the current view and selected items.

8 Use the buttons in the top left corner of the Photoshop application to launch Mini Bridge and Bridge as needed. Note: this Br button does not copy the Mini Bridge selection to Bridge.

9 Double-click on thumbnails to open them in Photoshop, or drag images from Mini Bridge to the editing area to combine.

10 Ctrl-click/right-click an image to show a menu of options, including Add to Favorites. Click a single image; Shift-click or Command-click/Ctrl-click to select multiples.

 HOT TIP: The Boomerang button in Bridge brings you back to Photoshop and updates Mini Bridge with your current view and selected items, just like the Br button in Mini Bridge updates Bridge.

▶ **SEE ALSO:** The grey band at the top of the Content area (7) has icons for Select, Filter items by rating, Sort, and Tools. The two icons to the right of the Br button are the Panel View and Search button. These features are equivalent to those in Bridge and will be covered later in this chapter.

Set Mini Bridge panel view and settings

1 Click the Panel View icon in the upper right section of the panel.

2 Click as needed to tick off both Path Bar and Navigation Pod.

3 Select Settings from the panel menu in the upper right corner.

4 Notice the Reset Preferences button in the lower left corner.

5 Click the Bridge Launching icon to set options as you like.

6 Click the Settings icon in the Path Bar.

7 Click the Appearance icon.

8 Be sure that the box marked Color Manage Panel is ticked.

9 Adjust user interface brightness and image backdrop as you like.

10 Click the Browse Files icon at the extreme right end of the Path Bar.

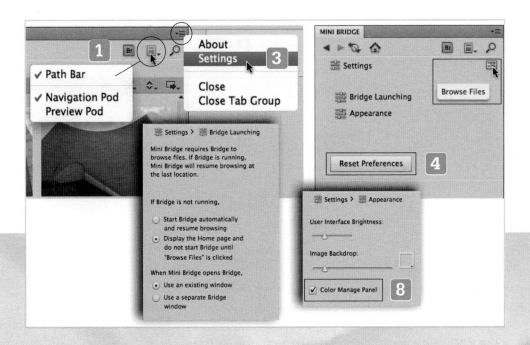

Go to Bridge from Photoshop

Though Mini Bridge is a useful and efficient tool for browsing images right within Photoshop, there will be times when you want the more robust feature set of Adobe Bridge. Additionally, Mini Bridge relies on the resources of Bridge. For these reasons, Photoshop offers a number of ways to launch and switch to Bridge.

1 Click the Br button in Mini Bridge to go to Bridge.

If you are browsing files in Mini Bridge, clicking this button will duplicate your current selection in Bridge. If Bridge is not running, clicking this button will start Bridge and then switch to it.

2 Click the Br button at the top of the Photoshop window to Launch Bridge and switch to it, ignoring your Mini Bridge selection.

3 If you quit Bridge or it crashes during your session, Mini Bridge will display a message. Click OK to restart Bridge.

4 Click the Boomerang icon to return to Photoshop from Bridge. Mini Bridge will update to match the current selection of images in Bridge.

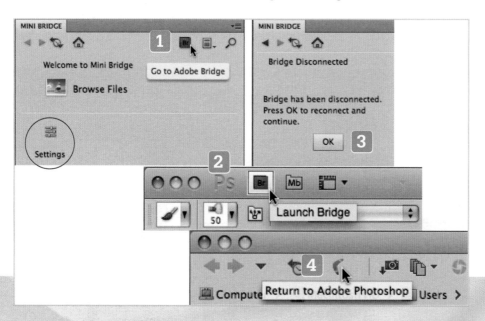

 HOT TIP: Because Bridge uses system resources such as memory and can take time to start up, you can set preferences for when it starts. To do this, click on Settings and then on Bridge Launching in the Mini Bridge panel.

Set key preferences in Bridge

To display the Preferences dialogue, select Adobe Bridge CS5, Preferences …
(Windows: Edit, Preferences …) from the menu bar. The preferences listed below are
mostly optional, with the recommended ones indicated. This list is intended more to let
you know where to locate these features, should you need them. The illustration shows
a tooltip in action.

1 Click on an item in the box on the left-hand side
of the dialogue to activate that preference page.

2 Tick off the relevant options in all pages of the
dialogue before clicking OK.

Some noteworthy preferences:

> ▶ **SEE ALSO:** You can set
> preferences for Camera
> Raw from Bridge. Details
> on setting Camera Raw
> preferences are given in
> Chapter 1.

- General page: When a Camera is Connected, Launch Adobe Photo Downloader; note
  the button to Reset All Warning Dialogues.
- Thumbnails page: Show Tooltips.
- Labels Page: note that the label names are editable.
- Cache page: Keep 100% previews in Cache; Automatically Export Cache to Folders
  When Possible (recommended); note the buttons – Compact Cache and Purge Cache.
- Advanced page: Start Bridge at Login, Generate Monitor-Size Previews.
- Output page: Preserve Embedded Color Profile (recommended); note the button to
  Reset Panel to Defaults.

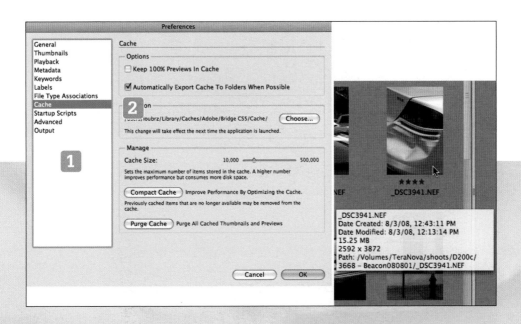

Use key elements of Bridge

This section will briefly cover some of the more salient features of Bridge. The Bridge workspace is divided into five main areas, consisting of three vertical columns to hold panels, a header and footer. In the example shown, the panels have been significantly rearranged from any of the default workspaces.

1 Use the Folders tab to navigate the files and folders on your computer. You can save a favourite for any folder or drive from this tab and use the Favorites tab to return to them. The Collections tab contains what are essentially virtual folders. Once you create a collection, you can drag files from multiple locations into them. Use the Filter tab to narrow the selection of files appearing in the Content panel based on metadata that you have assigned, such as a star rating.

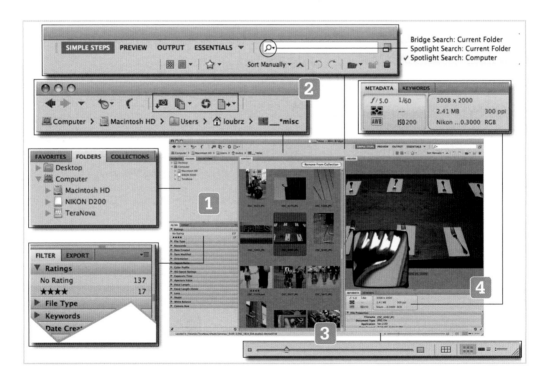

2 The left side of the header contains navigation tools and the Boomerang button, which switches you back to Photoshop. There are also buttons for Photo Downloader, the Review menu, Opening in Camera Raw, and switching to the Output module. The right side contains the Workspace Switcher and the Search box. A Filter menu allows you to narrow your selection of images, while the Sort menu allows you to control the sequence of the thumbnails in the Content panel.

3 The Content panel can show thumbnails in a number of layouts. When browsing collections, it includes a button that allows you to remove images from the collection. Aside from using the Sort menu, you can drag thumbnails to sequence them. The footer contains a status line and a slider to set the size of the thumbnails.

4 You can size the preview panel to show a lot of detail, or hide it completely. When you click in the preview panel, the Loupe tool will magnify the area around the point that you clicked. The Metadata and Keywords panels allow you to view and manage descriptive data attached to your files.

 HOT TIP: Bridge can only browse media on volumes that are connected to the computer. When you disconnect from that network server or eject that disc, its thumbnails and previews go away. This is different from a cataloguing tool like Lightroom's Library module, which gathers up thumbnails and previews of the discs it scans and stores them in an image database. When you eject the disc from Lightroom, you can still browse the information in its database. There are advantages and disadvantages to each approach.

Arrange, save and reset workspaces

Bridge is highly configurable, though not quite as flexible as the Photoshop workspace. As in Photoshop, workspaces are live. Once you save a workspace, Bridge will remember any further adjustments to the workspace arrangement until you reset it. Unlike Photoshop, you can't drag tabs around to reorder them within a group or float panels.

1 Resize columns and panels by dragging their edges.

2 Panels can be dragged between columns, stacked on top of each other, or nested in tab groups. The feedback is similar to what you get in Photoshop.

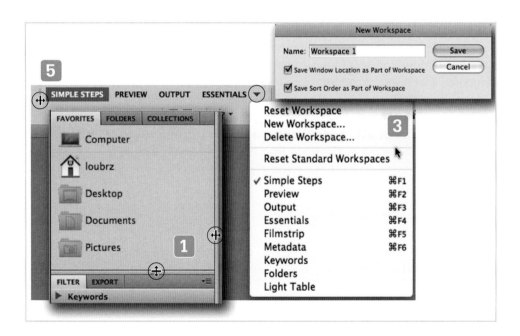

3 To save a workspace, press down on the triangle and select New Workspace ... from the menu. Enter a name, and note that your workspace can remember the window location and sort order. Click Save.

4 To reset workspaces:

- Choose Reset Workspace or Reset Standard Workspaces from the Workspace Switcher menu.
- Ctrl-click/right-click on a button in the Workspace Switcher and choose Reset from the menu.

5 To rearrange the Workspace Switcher:

- Drag the dashed double vertical line at the left edge to expand or shrink it.
- Drag a button to a new location. A blue line will appear to show where the button will land.
- To insert a workspace button, Ctrl-click/right-click on a button in the Workspace Switcher and choose a workspace from the menu.

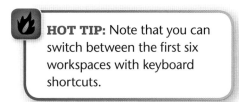

HOT TIP: Note that you can switch between the first six workspaces with keyboard shortcuts.

Navigate with folders and favourites

1 Click the triangle next to an icon in the Folders panel to expand or collapse its sub-folders.

2 Click on an icon in the Folders panel to browse its contents.

3 Double-click on folder icons in the content window to browse their content.

4 Use the Go Back/Go Forward buttons or select an item from the Recent Files and Folders menu to revisit recently browsed locations.

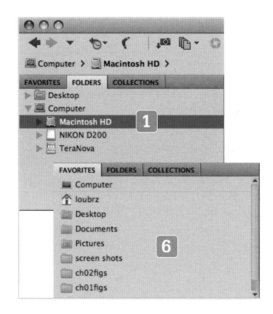

 ALERT: The Path Bar can be hidden. If you don't see it, choose Path Bar from the Window menu.

 HOT TIP: The Parents and Favorites menu combines the contents of the Path Bar and the Favorites panel.

5 Click on an icon in the Path Bar or select from the Parents and Favourites menu to go to that location.

6 Click on an item in the Favorites tab to browse that location.

7 To add a favourite, Ctrl-click/right-click on an item in the Content panel and select Add to Favorites from the menu.

8 To remove a favourite, Ctrl-click/right-click on an item in the Favorites panel and select Remove from Favorites.

9 Click the Boomerang button to switch to Photoshop and continue browsing the current location with Mini Bridge.

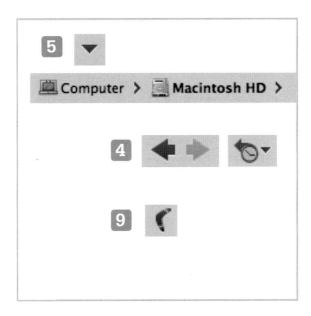

Browse images in Bridge

Any of the previously mentioned navigation techniques, performing a search or clicking on a collection will result in a set of images that appear in the Content panel.

1 Click on a thumbnail to view it in the Preview panel and hit the space bar for a full-screen preview. Hit the space bar again to exit full screen.

2 Click in the Preview panel to activate the Loupe tool. (There may be a slight delay while the tool starts up.) Drag the Loupe to view different parts of the image. Click on the Loupe again to put it away.

3 Drag images to sort manually, or use the Sort menu.

4 To rotate images, click on the image and then click the Rotate icons in the Path Bar or use Command/Ctrl + [to rotate anti-clockwise and Command/Ctrl +] to rotate clockwise.

5 Click on the items in the Filter panel to show or hide thumbnails in the Content panel. A tick appears next to active filters. Click on the item again to switch it off. You can also activate multiple filters at the same time.

6 To select more than one image, click the first thumbnail, then Shift-click on another to select it and all images between the first and second; or Command/Ctrl-click each additional image that you want to select. You can also Command/Ctrl-click to deselect one of several images that have already been selected.

HOT TIP: Bridge places indicator badges in the Content panel next to images that have been adjusted or cropped.

HOT TIP: Sometimes, all you need to find an image quickly is a layout with lots of thumbnails. If you hit the Tab key, Bridge will expand the current Content panel and hide away all others. Hit the Tab key again, and you return to the previous view.

Use organisation features: collections and filters

Favourites and folder browsing are very useful, but they can only show you files from a single folder at a time. You can do a search across an entire drive, but the search can take time and return many more results than you want. Collections are essentially virtual folders that allow you to drag files from anywhere and drop them in. The collection only keeps a reference to the file, instead of making a copy. If you move a file after you have added it to a collection, Bridge gives you a way to update the reference.

Whenever you browse a group of images, Bridge compiles statistics about them in the Filter panel. Filtering can be applied to searches, folders or collections.

1 To create a new collection, click the New Collection button at the bottom of the Collections panel. If any files are selected, you will be asked if you want to include them in the new collection. Enter a name for the collection and hit the Return/Enter key to accept.

2 To remove a file from a collection, click to select it and then click Remove from Collection.

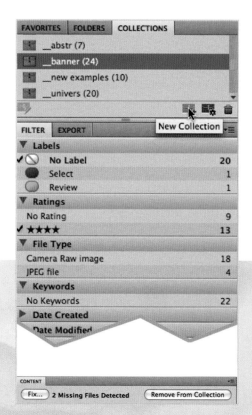

3 To delete a collection, click on it and then click on the dustbin icon in the Collections panel.

4 Click on an item in the Filter panel to activate it. A tick mark will appear on its left side.

5 To combine filters, click on several items.

6 To cancel a filter, click on it again.

7 If Bridge reports missing files detected:

- Click Fix ... The location of the missing file will appear in a dialogue box.
- If the file is moved, click Browse ... (You can also click Skip or Remove, depending on the circumstances.)
- The old location of the missing file will appear at the top of the browsing dialogue.
- Navigate to the file in its new location and press Open.
- This cycle repeats until all missing files are resolved, though you can cancel at any time.

Apply ratings, labels, keywords and IPTC data

You can embed a wealth of information into your image using IPTC data. Select one or more files, and then apply your metadata as needed, using the Metadata panel or the File Info dialogue.

1 Use the Label menu or keyboard shortcuts to apply star ratings and labels.

2 Click in the fields with pencils next to them and enter data.

3 When you are done, click the tick icon to apply.

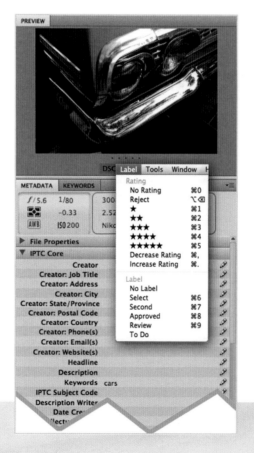

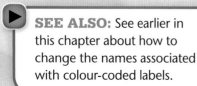

SEE ALSO: See earlier in this chapter about how to change the names associated with colour-coded labels.

Make a slideshow

The Slideshow feature is a convenient way to put together an ad-hoc presentation. If none of the files in the Content panel is selected, Slideshow will show all of the files in your Content panel. Use Shift-click or Command/Ctrl-click to select specific files to show. You can also drag files to sequence them. When you have your files sequenced and selected, do the following:

1 Select View, Slideshow Options ... from the menu bar (Shift + Command/Ctrl + L).

2 Set your desired preferences.

3 Click Play.

4 Hit the space bar to pause or resume.

5 Use keyboard shortcuts to add labels and ratings while the slideshow is running.

6 Hit Shift + Command/Ctrl + L during the slideshow to adjust preferences on the fly. The slideshow will resume.

7 Hit Esc to end the slideshow.

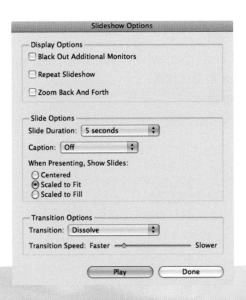

HOT TIP: You don't always have to open the Slideshow preferences to begin a slideshow. Once you've set your preferences, you can start the slideshow directly with Command/Ctrl + L. The slideshow will use the same preferences the next time.

HOT TIP: Collections are great for organising files for slideshows you want to present more than once.

Go to Camera Raw or Photoshop from Bridge

When you double-click an image in Bridge or Mini Bridge, it is automatically opened with the appropriate tool, either Camera Raw or Photoshop. Since Camera Raw can edit JPEG and TIFF files, you might want to force those files into Camera Raw instead of having them open by default in Photoshop.

1 In Bridge or Mini Bridge, Ctrl-click/right-click on an image to display a menu; choose Open in Camera Raw ... or Open with Default Application.

2 In Bridge, use Command/Ctrl + R to open in Camera Raw.

3 To force all files to always open in Camera Raw:

- Choose Adobe Bride CS5, Camera Raw Preferences (Windows: Edit, Camera Raw Preferences) from the menu bar.
- Choose Automatically open all supported JPEGs and Automatically open all supported TIFFs from the menus in the JPEG and TIFF handling section.
- Click OK.

ALERT: If you select Disable JPEG or TIFF support from the menus in the JPEG and TIFF handling section, you will not be able to open any JPEG or TIFF files in Camera Raw, even those with settings.

HOT TIP: Camera Raw only supports flat TIFF files. It cannot edit TIFF files with layers.

3 Pre-edit in Camera Raw

Introduction

Adobe Camera Raw is a plug-in that translates the raw data captured from a camera's image sensor into a digital image that Photoshop can edit. The plug-in extends the functionality of both Photoshop and Bridge.

Camera Raw is very powerful, and is even sufficient to make great images without opening them in Photoshop proper, but a good way to think of it is as a pre-processor that can do a lot of the initial leg-work in making an image look great before you do open them in Photoshop, saving you a lot of work.

The advantages of shooting in Raw over shooting in JPEG are increased dynamic range and the flexibility to remake critical technical decisions, such as white balance, after the fact. While Camera Raw was initially designed specifically for raw data, its interface and non-destructive editing system make it a good tool for pre-processing JPEG and TIFF files as well.

With Creative Suite 5, Adobe is introducing Camera Raw 6, a major rewrite of the Camera Raw 'engine' that processes high-ISO images with dramatically less noise, better detail and higher quality colour.

If you are familiar with Lightroom, Camera Raw is the functional equivalent of Lightroom's Develop module. In fact, Adobe went out of its way to make sure that all of the tools in each product match up.

Open a file in Camera Raw from Bridge or Mini Bridge

When you double-click on a raw file, it will automatically open in Camera Raw. To open JPEG or TIFF files in Camera Raw, do one of the following:

1 In Bridge, click on the Open in Camera Raw icon.

2 Ctrl-click/right-click on the thumbnail and select Open in Camera Raw ... from the menu.

3 With the Camera Raw preferences set accordingly, double-click on a JPEG or TIFF file to open it in Camera Raw.

> ▶ **SEE ALSO:** Set preferences for Adobe Camera Raw in Chapter 1.

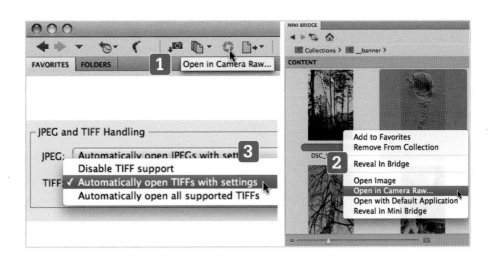

> ⚠ **ALERT:** Camera Raw cannot read layered TIFF files. If JPEG and TIFF support are disabled in Camera Raw, it will not open JPEG or TIFF files, even when they contain settings.

> 🔥 **HOT TIP:** Every camera has a different raw format. When manufacturers come out with new cameras, Adobe Camera Raw and even the operating system you are working with have to be updated to be able to use and display the content from those files. If you have just got a newly released camera and can't use your raw files with Photoshop, check the Adobe website for an update.

Use the Adobe Camera Raw interface

This section is a quick survey of the elements of the Camera Raw environment, listed clockwise from the upper left. Keyboard shortcuts for some of the controls are listed below. Detailed discussion of many of these tools will come later in the chapter.

1 Tool bar, including rotate image buttons. Click the buttons or type L or R to rotate left or right, respectively.

2 Toggle preview (P) and full-screen (F) controls.

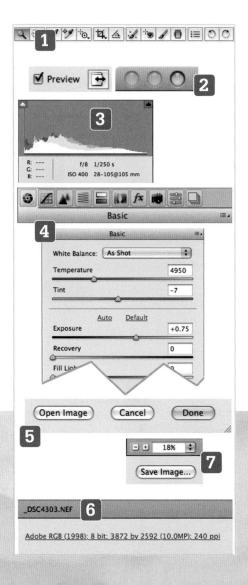

3 Histogram and info readout. The histogram includes clipping warnings for shadow/underexposure (U) and highlight/overexposure (O).

4 Adjustment panels are organised by a series of settings tabs that are labelled with icons. Hover the mouse pointer over a tab to see a tooltip describing it.

5 Open Image, Cancel and Done buttons.

6 Workflow settings link.

7 Save Image button and zoom control.

HOT TIP: On the Mac, the green button in the upper left corner of the dialogue is a second full-screen button.

Set workflow options

Even though the preview you see in Camera Raw looks like an image, it's not – yet. A raw file is like unprocessed film, and Camera Raw is the digital developer. When you click the Open button, Camera Raw applies your workflow settings and adjustments to a copy of the raw data and hands off the adjusted image to Photoshop.

Your current workflow settings appear as underlined text at the bottom of the dialogue. These settings determine the colour space, bit depth and resolution that the file will have in Photoshop. These settings are 'sticky', meaning that they will remain as you set them until you change them again. The settings shown in this example are recommended for general purpose photo editing.

1 Click the text to open the Workflow Options dialogue.

2 Set Space to Adobe RGB.

3 Set Depth to 16 Bits/Channel.

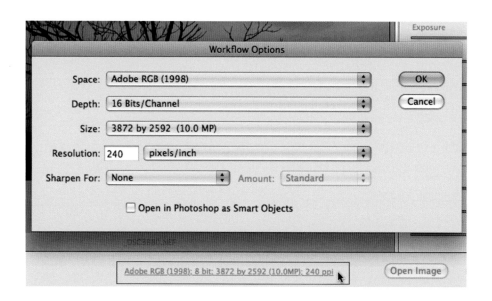

4 Use native size. The dimensions vary by camera, but the native size does not have either a + (plus sign) or a 2 (minus sign) to the right of it.

5 Resolution is not critical in this dialogue: 240 or 300 pixels/inch is normal.

6 Set Sharpen For to None (sharpening will be applied later in Photoshop).

7 Leave Open in Photoshop as Smart Objects unticked, unless you have a special purpose for using that feature.

8 Click OK.

9 Note that the underlined text in the Camera Raw dialogue has updated to reflect your choices.

WHAT DOES THIS MEAN?

8 bits/pixel and 16 bits/pixel: known as colour depth or bit depth, these determine how many colours can be in an image. Generally, it's best to work in 16 bits, as that gives more latitude to make tonal adjustments without causing colour gradients to break into bands of flat colour.

Prophoto RGB: a special colour space that holds an enormous range of potential colours – including colours that your monitor literally cannot display. It should only be used in 16-bit mode.

 HOT TIP: Resolution only comes into play when you are printing. The resolution that you set here only affects the default size at which the image will be printed, and you can easily change it later.

Use adjustment tabs

Most of the work of Camera Raw is done with sliding controls that are grouped into tabbed panels. Hover the mouse pointer over a tab to see its name in a tooltip.

1 Basic: includes white balance, exposure, vibrance.

2 Tone curves: parametric and point curves can be used together.

3 Detail: noise reduction and sharpening.

4 HSL/Grayscale: colour adjustments and black and white conversion.

5 Split toning.

6 Lens correction: lens defringing and lens vignetting.

7 Effects: grain and post-crop vignetting.

8 Camera calibration: includes process and camera profiles.

9 Presets.

10 Snapshots.

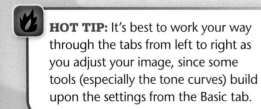

HOT TIP: It's best to work your way through the tabs from left to right as you adjust your image, since some tools (especially the tone curves) build upon the settings from the Basic tab.

Zoom in or out

There are several ways to zoom in and out in the Camera Raw dialogue. Most of these techniques also work in Photoshop.

1 Click the + or − buttons in the lower left corner of the display area.

2 Click on the blue button in the lower left corner and choose a zoom level from the menu.

3 Click the magnifying glass tool (in the upper left corner of the dialogue), then click in the image to zoom in or Option/Alt-click to zoom out.

4 Drag the magnifying glass tool diagonally in the image to surround a detail. That section of the image will expand to fill the display area.

5 Hold the Command/Ctrl key and tap the − (plus) key to zoom in.

6 Hold Command/Ctrl and tap − (minus) to zoom out.

7 Hold Command/Ctrl and tap 0 (zero) to fit in the window.

8 Hold Shift + Command/Ctrl and tap 0 (zero) to zoom to 100%.

 HOT TIP: When you are zoomed in, hold the space bar to switch to the hand tool and drag to view other parts of the image.

Crop an image or remove cropping

Use cropping to reframe your image. Aside from free form (Normal mode) cropping, the Crop tool in Camera Raw has pre-set aspect ratios that match classic camera formats, and you can specify your own custom shape as well. Cropping in Camera Raw is non-destructive, like all other Camera Raw adjustments.

1 Optional: Choose Custom ... from the menu and enter a proportion (e.g. 16 to 9) or select a pre-set proportion like 1 to 1.

2 Hold the mouse button down in the image area and drag out a rough selection. (Notice that Camera Raw has dimmed the part of the image outside the cropped area when you release the mouse button.)

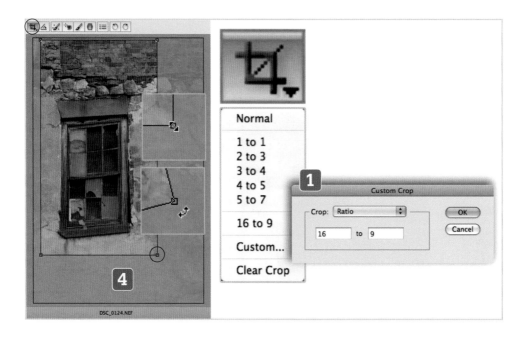

HOT TIP: If you change your mind about cropping and you haven't committed the cropped area, you can hit the Esc key to cancel.

SEE ALSO: If you crop in Photoshop, you can evaluate the composition with a Rule of Thirds grid. See Chapter 9.

3 Hold the mouse button down inside the cropped area and drag to reposition it.

4 To scale or rotate, position the mouse pointer so that the cursor changes to the appropriate shape and then drag. The cursor will change shape depending on whether it is directly over or slightly outside one of the handles.

5 Hit the Return key to commit the crop.

6 To remove cropping from an image, choose Clear Crop from the menu.

? DID YOU KNOW?

Most digital SLRs produce images with the same proportions as 35 mm film: 2 to 3. The most common aspect ratios in still cameras are 2 to 3, 3 to 4, and 1 to 1. The 16 to 9 aspect ratio is standard for HDTV and European digital television. However, other aspect ratios are worth consideration.

Basic tab: adjust White Balance and Tint

The White Balance and Tint controls work together to neutralise two aspects of light that produce colour casts in a photo. They shift the colours in the image so that the areas that are supposed to be neutral grey come out that way, and the rest of the colours fall in line.

To get the most neutral colour, some photographers intentionally shoot a special grey target for use with the White Balance tool in Camera Raw. On the other hand, there may be times when you want to push the white balance intentionally to create a more artistic result. Here are some approaches to using White Balance:

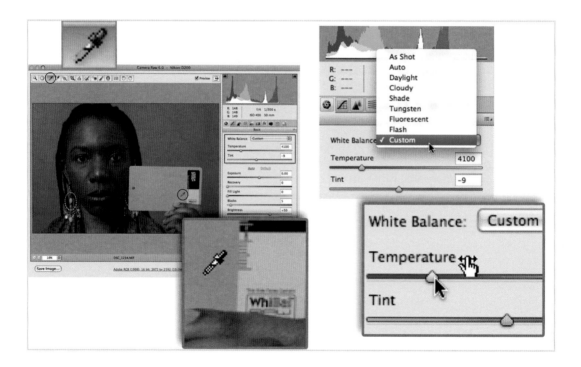

SEE ALSO: White balance and other settings from one raw file can be applied to other files. See Open multiple images and synchronise white balance, etc. later in this chapter.

HOT TIP: You can use the white balance adjustment with JPEG and TIFF files, but there are no pre-set options with these files, as there are with raw files.

1. Try different pre-sets in the White Balance menu. Notice that each pre-set changes the shape of the histogram and assigns different settings to the Temperature and Tint sliders.

2. Click on the White Balance tool in the upper left portion of the Camera Raw interface, then click on a grey target or click on an area in your image that should be neutral grey. The new white balance will be set.

3. If you don't like the result, try clicking somewhere else. Clicking on things that are warm-toned in real life will impart a cool tone to the image, and clicking on things that are cool-toned in real life will impart a warm tone to the image.

4. Once you establish a neutral white balance for your image, you can then intentionally warm it or cool it by shifting the white balance – for example, you could set each image to 200K above its neutral white point.

5. Try a mix of approaches: you can start with a pre-set, and then move the Temperature slider. As you move the Temperature slider to the right, your image will take on a progressively more yellow–orange tone. If you move it to the left, the image will become increasingly blue.

Straighten an image

The Straighten tool is really an extension of the Crop tool. It allows you to define what is vertical or horizontal in your picture, and then rotates and crops the image so that the sides are square. Like the Crop tool in Camera Raw, Straighten is reversible.

1 Drag a dotted line with the tool to indicate either the horizon line or a line that should be perfectly vertical.

2 The Crop tool will become active when you release the mouse button.

3 As with the Crop tool before, you can use the corner handles to resize the crop, and you can drag the crop area.

4 Hit the Return key to accept the crop.

5 To remove straightening, choose Clear Crop from the Crop Tool menu.

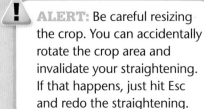

SEE ALSO: Straightening an image always leaves gaps on the edges because the scene is rotated. Instead of cropping those gaps away as you do in Camera Raw, you can crop in Photoshop and leave the gaps. Then, you can use Content-Aware fill to construct new edges.

ALERT: Be careful resizing the crop. You can accidentally rotate the crop area and invalidate your straightening. If that happens, just hit Esc and redo the straightening.

Basic tab: adjust Exposure, Recovery, Fill Light, etc.

This set of controls allows you to adjust the tonality of your image. Typically, it is best to work from top to bottom with these controls. Notice how the histogram changes shape as you move the slider. You can use these controls with the clipping warnings – toggle them by clicking on them or by tapping U to show clipped shadows in blue and O to show clipped highlights in red.

Raw files have a significant amount of latitude, allowing you to recover detail in blown highlights and blocked shadows. Highlight recovery is not possible with JPEGs or TIFFs.

1 Move the Exposure slider to lighten or darken all tones in the image. At some point, parts of the image will look either too light or too dark.

2 If you have 'blown' highlights (pure white and missing detail), you may be able to restore detail with the Recovery slider. Move the slider to the right by degrees until you see the details appear. Notice that at higher settings, some middle tones are also affected.

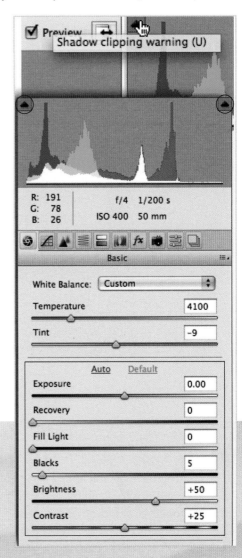

HOT TIP: Toggle the Preview tick box on and off as you adjust the image to check your progress. It's not always easy to gauge when your adjustments have gone too far.

3 Use the Fill Light control to lighten details in the shadows. It can 'open up' shadow details that are 'blocked'.

4 The Blacks slider works somewhat differently from Fill Light and can add substance to a photo that doesn't have any pure blacks, or it can reduce the heaviness of an image by lightening all of the dark elements.

5 Use the Brightness slider to adjust the upper middle tones the most. It makes the overall image brighter, but does not shift the shadows and the brightest parts of the image as quickly as the Exposure slider.

6 Use the Contrast slider to increase or decrease the difference between light and dark values. Move the slider both left and right to gauge its effect.

? DID YOU KNOW?

Clipping isn't always a bad thing. Sometimes the drama of a photo lies in the fact that part of it is plunged into complete blackness, or that there is a bright spot of pure white light in the midst of it. Let the indicators advise you, but not control you.

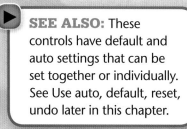

SEE ALSO: These controls have default and auto settings that can be set together or individually. See Use auto, default, reset, undo later in this chapter.

Basic tab: adjust Clarity, Vibrance, Saturation

These three controls have to do with the richness or purity of the colours in your image. Clarity increases contrast in a targeted way. Vibrance increases saturation, but protects skin tones and affects already saturated colours more gradually. For most purposes, Vibrance is a better choice than Saturation when you want to increase the purity of the colours.

1 Move the Clarity slider to the right until you begin to see broad haloes appear around the edges of your details, then move the slider slightly to the left until the haloes vanish.

2 Move the Vibrance slider to the right or left to increase or decrease saturation respectively. Notice how skin tones and saturated colours respond and that hints of colour remain in the image when you move the slider all the way to the left.

3 Move the Saturation slider to increase or decrease saturation. Notice how the colours change, and that it is easy to produce unpleasant over-saturated skin colours.

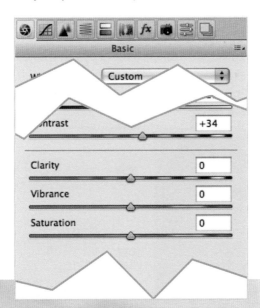

 HOT TIP: When using the Clarity control, it is generally best to zoom in to 100% or more first. This is true for many of the controls that affect detail.

 SEE ALSO: You can make a black and white image by pulling the Saturation slider all the way to the left, but a better way is to tick the convert box in the HSL/Grayscale tab. It works like the Black and White adjustment covered on p. 239.

Use the preview and slider controls

Toggling the preview on and off as you work is a good way to evaluate whether your adjustments are improving the image.

All of the slider controls in Camera Raw, and Photoshop in general, have numerous ways of operating them beyond dragging the slider. Knowing these techniques can save you a lot of mousing around.

1 Hit the P key to toggle the tick in the Preview box.

2 Click in the value fields and use the up or down arrow keys to adjust the values in small increments. Use Shift + arrow key to adjust in larger increments.

3 Click on the label of a slider to select its input field. Type a new value.

4 Hold the mouse button down on a label and drag right or left to use the 'scrubby slider' to change the value of the field.

5 Click on the slider bar, and the thumb will snap to where you clicked.

6 After you use the scrubby slider or click on the slider bar, the field will still be selected. You can use the up or down arrow keys to make further adjustments.

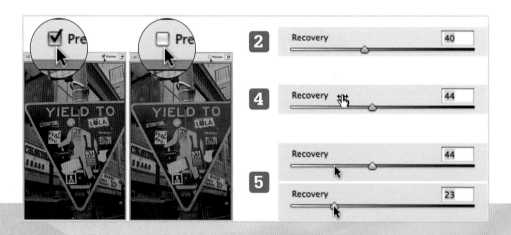

ALERT: When a blinking cursor or highlighted text is inside a value box, that field is said to have 'focus'. This can sometimes interfere with keyboard shortcuts because the field soaks up the keystroke. You may see your typing appear in the field, but at other times Photoshop will just beep. Hit Return/ Enter to commit changes to the field and take the focus off the field.

Use Auto, Default, Reset, Undo

In the Basic tab, you will see the words Auto and Default underlined. These are useful buttons designed to behave like web hyperlinks – the text in the link is shown in grey when that mode is active. The HSL/Grayscale tab has a Default button that works the same way.

1 Click Auto to have Camera Raw determine the settings for you. It often does a good job, and you can adjust the settings further, once you have applied auto settings.

2 Click Default to return all sliders to their default settings.

3 If you want to return an individual slider to its default setting, double-click on it.

4 If you want to have Camera Raw to set the value for a slider automatically, hold the Shift key down and double-click the slider.

5 To reset all of the settings for the file, hold down the Option/Alt key – the Cancel button will become a Reset button. Click the button, and then release the Option/Alt key.

6 You can use Undo (Command/Ctrl + Z) to reverse any slider changes and even the Reset button.

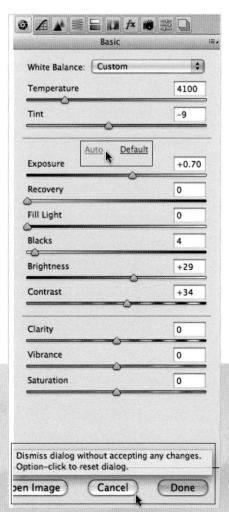

Use presets and snapshots

Presets lets you name a set of adjustments and store them for reuse with other images, while snapshots allows you to store several variations of settings within a single image. When you open other images in Camera Raw, you'll be able to apply any presets you have created, but you won't see snapshots for any other images. Snapshots remain in the image until you delete them.

1 To make a new preset, click the Presets tab.

2 Click the icon that looks like a turned-up page to add a new preset.

3 Use the subset menu or click on check boxes to tick off the adjustments you want to record in the preset.

4 Enter a name and click OK to save.

5 To make a new snapshot, click the Snapshots tab.

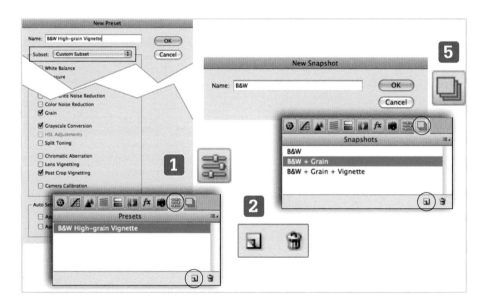

6 Click the icon that looks like a turned-up page to add a new snapshot.

7 Enter a name and click OK to save.

8 To use a preset or snapshot, click the tab and then click on its name in the list.

To delete a preset or snapshot:

9 Click the tab, and then click on the preset or snapshot.

10 Click the dustbin icon.

> **! ALERT:** After you delete a snapshot or preset, its settings will still be in effect. If you want to clear those settings, change the settings by hand, click another preset or snapshot, or reset the dialogue.

Add grain, post-crop vignetting

Digital noise is something that we try to eliminate, but film grain, especially in black and white images, can be aesthetically pleasing. Photographers took advantage of the Lens Vignetting tool in previous versions, but that had to be readjusted if you changed the cropping. Post-crop vignetting automatically reapplies the vignette effect after you crop an image or remove the crop.

1 Click the Effects tab.

2 Zoom in to evaluate the grain effect.

3 Use the sliders to create your grain effect.

4 Choose Fit in View from the size menu or hit Command/Ctrl + 0 (zero) to evaluate the vignetting.

5 Slide the amount to the left or right to darken or lighten respectively.

6 Choose a style from the menu to alter how the vignette affects colours and tones in the image.

7 Adjust Midpoint, Roundness, Feather and Highlights to adjust the character of the vignette.

HOT TIP: Midpoint doesn't have to do with location in the image; the vignette is always drawn from the centre. Midpoint has to do with the steepness of the transition in the vignette. A low value affects more of the image.

Reset, cancel or save settings without opening Photoshop

In some workflows (e.g. when making a quick web gallery or PDF) you may need to make adjustments in Camera Raw for the moment, and put the images aside for later. In other cases, you need to start over from scratch with your settings, or exit Camera Raw without updating the settings.

1 To save your adjustments without opening Photoshop, click the Done button or hit the Return/Enter key.

2 To discard your adjustments, click the Cancel button or hit the Esc key.

3 To reset the dialogue, hold down the Option/Alt key – the Cancel button will become a Reset button – and click the Reset button.

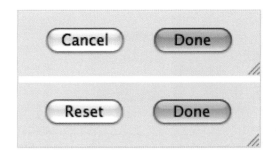

Open multiple images and synchronise white balance, etc.

You can select multiple images in Bridge and open them in Camera Raw. The images appear in a vertical strip on the left side of the dialogue. You can then edit images individually or select several and adjust them as a group, and you can synchronise settings between multiple files. Once you have synchronised settings, you can click on individual images to adjust them further, save your images, exit the dialogue and save your adjustments, or even open one or more files in Photoshop.

1 Select multiple images in Bridge, using Shift-click or Command/Ctrl-click.

2 Click the Open in Camera Raw icon or use Command/Ctrl + R.

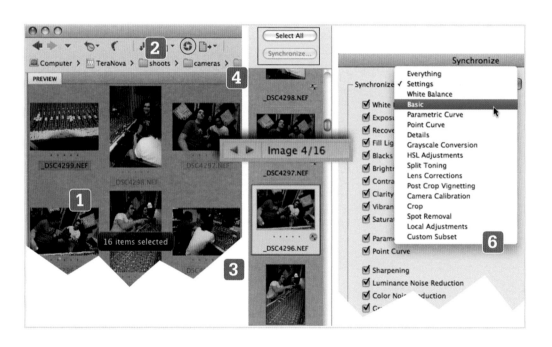

To synchronise settings:

3 Click on your reference image (e.g. one containing a white balance target) to establish settings such as white balance, exposure, black and white conversion, etc.

4 Click Select All or use Command/Ctrl + A to select all images in the group, or use Shift-click or Command/Ctrl-click to select additional images to sync.

5 Click Synchronize …

6 Use the Synchronize menu or tick off the boxes to select the settings you want to synchronise.

7 Click OK.

 HOT TIP: Once you have synchronised and adjusted your images, click Save Images… to export JPEGS, TIFFs, etc. or click Done to exit the dialogue and save the adjustments. If you click Cancel, none of the changes will be recorded. You can also select one or more images and open them directly into Photoshop, or switch to the Output module to save a web gallery or PDF.

 ALERT: Camera Raw will allow you to open and adjust a lot of images at once. If you click Open Images, you may get a warning, but Photoshop will try to open them all. The result can be very sluggish performance. It's OK to open more than one image at once from Camera Raw, but it's best to open only a few.

Use Open Image

With all the processing power in Camera Raw, there is still much more that can be done in Photoshop. The button marked Open Image is really three buttons – Open Image, Open a Copy, and Open Object. Each behaves in a slightly different way, but in each case, Camera Raw will apply the settings to a copy of the raw data. It then converts the image according to the workflow options and hands that adjusted copy over to Photoshop.

1 Click the Open Image button to open the adjusted image in Photoshop. Your settings will be updated in the XMP data.

2 Hold down the Option/Alt key – the Open Image button changes to Open a Copy – and click. The adjusted image will open in Photoshop, but the current settings will be discarded. This preserves the previous settings stored in the XMP data.

3 Hold down the Shift key – the Open Image button changes to Open Object – and click. The current settings will be applied, the XMP data will be updated, and a copy of the source file will be embedded as a smart object into the file that Photoshop receives.

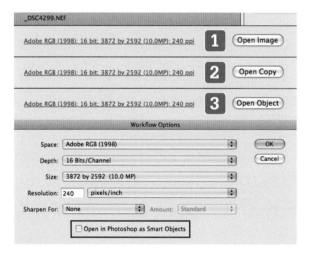

 DID YOU KNOW?
Open a Copy can be used when you want to process the same file several different ways in Camera Raw (e.g. once for the highlights and a second time for the shadows) and then composite pieces of the various versions together in Photoshop.

 SEE ALSO: Since Open a Copy discards your settings when you multi-process a file, it can be helpful to use snapshots (use Open Image instead of Open a Copy) to store each version of the conversion. That makes it easier to repeat, if you have to. See Use presets and snapshots earlier in this chapter.

 HOT TIP: If Open in Photoshop as Smart Objects is ticked in your workflow options (not recommended), the Open Image button will be labelled Open Object, and holding the Shift key down will convert it to Open Image.

 ALERT: Use Open Object with care, especially when editing raw files. It is a useful feature, but embedding a raw file in your Photoshop document can dramatically increase its size and slow performance.

4 Save files and manage colours

Introduction

This chapter is here because saving files is an often-overlooked topic. It is worth stating explicitly up-front that you should save your file repeatedly as you work on it. There are also some subtleties to saving files that are worth explaining. Photoshop's ability to edit images would be of limited value if it could only save files in one or two formats. One of its strengths is that it can read and write so many formats, including some uncommon ones. Thus, beyond being an excellent editing tool, it can be a platform for translating between image formats as well.

When we think in terms of workflow, there is often a progression of files that get created and saved along the way to your finished image. It might begin as a raw or JPEG file from your camera, or as a scanned TIFF file. Once you bring the file into Photoshop, it's time to save your work-in-process file, which would typically be a Photoshop PSD file. From there, you might save a low-resolution JPEG to use as an e-mail attachment, a high-resolution TIFF file to print promotional cards at a service bureau, or even a separate PSD file that is optimised for printing on a large-scale ink-jet or giclée printer.

When you're saving files for the web or for printing at a service bureau, there are important colour management issues to consider. These will be discussed in this chapter as well.

SEE ALSO: Making PDFs and web galleries with Bridge is covered in Chapter 2. Camera Raw also has the Save Image button, which is discussed in Chapter 3.

Save a file as a Photoshop file

It's a good idea to save your work-in-progress files in Photoshop format. If you maintain a policy of only distributing JPEG and TIFF files, the .psd extension becomes a way of knowing at a glance whether a file is for your own internal work.

When you save files in Photoshop, the dialogues are actually being handled by your operating system, so your screens may look different from what you see here. However, the general functionality is the same. You should check your operating system documentation or system help for additional information.

1 Choose File, Save as ... from the menu bar.

2 In the dialogue, specify a name for the file.

3 Specify a location to save the file. You may need to navigate the dialogue to another folder or create a new folder from within the dialogue.

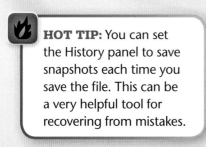

HOT TIP: You can set the History panel to save snapshots each time you save the file. This can be a very helpful tool for recovering from mistakes.

4 Make sure Photoshop is selected in the Format menu. (The extension will change to .psd if another format was selected earlier.)

5 For your work files, be sure that Alpha Channels and Layers are ticked.

6 Always embed the colour profile.

7 Optional: tick As a Copy. (See What does this mean? for details.)

8 Click Save.

WHAT DOES THIS MEAN?

File, Save: really a save and replace command. It deletes the previous version of a file and saves the new version in its place.

File, Save As …: allows you to specify a new name and/or location for your file. If a file has never been saved before, the File, Save command does the same thing as File, Save As …

As a Copy: useful for saving a file that works like a snapshot or a backup of your work in progress. Whenever you open a document in Photoshop, it becomes 'current'. When you choose File, Save, the current document gets saved and replaced. If you choose File, Save As …, two things happen: a file with a new name gets created, and that file becomes the new current document. You can override that behaviour by using File, Save As … and ticking As a Copy. That option lets you save a copy of a file without changing the current document.

For example, if you start working on a file called File01.psd and use File, Save As … to create File02.psd, then File02 will be replaced each subsequent time you choose File, Save. If you tick As a Copy when you create File02.psd with File, Save As…, then File01 will remain the current document and it will continue to be updated when you use File, Save. If you discover later on that you don't like some change that you made in File01 after you created File02, then you can discard File01 and resume work on File02.

 DID YOU KNOW?

If you combine lots of images, layers, smart objects, etc. into a single file, its size can exceed 2 GB, and you will get a warning from Photoshop telling you the file could not be saved. In that case, choose Large Document Format from the Format menu instead of Photoshop. The file will be saved with a .psb extension instead of .psd. A PSB file can hold 4,000 terabytes.

Save a file as a TIFF

TIFF files are popular in part because, unlike Photoshop files, they are based on a published format. As a result, most graphics software can read and write TIFF files and the format, along with PDF, has become a graphics industry standard. TIFF files are ideal for submitting your work to service bureaus for output. Service bureaus often require files that have been converted to one of the CMYK colour spaces. This subject will be discussed later in the chapter.

To save a TIFF file, begin as you would for a PSD: choose File, Save As ... from the menu bar and specify a name and location. Then, do the following:

1 Select TIFF from the Format menu.

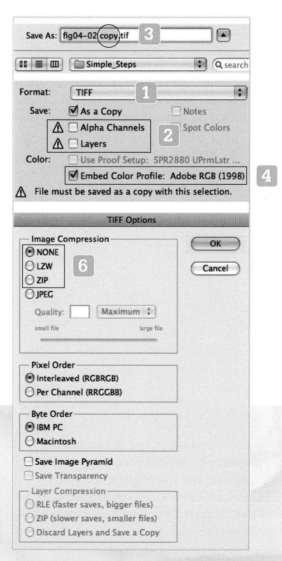

2 Untick Alpha Channels and Layers. This makes the file smaller and more portable. Photoshop will warn you that the file must be saved as a copy.

3 Photoshop has added the word 'copy' to your file name – change it, if you like.

4 Be sure to embed the colour profile.

5 Click Save. The TIFF Options dialogue will appear.

6 Optional: choose LZW or ZIP compression. (Avoid JPEG compression.)

7 You can ignore Pixel Order and Byte Order.

8 Click OK.

HOT TIP: Some software can't work with layered files. It's generally a good idea to untick Layers to flatten files if you're turning them over to someone else, especially if they're going to a service bureau. By the same token, some users can't work with compressed files either. It's always a good idea to check with the recipient before you send them a compressed or layered file.

ALERT: JPEG compression makes files smaller by throwing away data, and can dramatically degrade your image. If you want to use JPEG compression and you don't need layers, save the file as a JPEG, instead. LZW or ZIP compression can't shrink your TIFF file as much as JPEG but the files are identical to the originals when they are restored.

Convert or assign colour profiles

Converting between colour profiles can shift your colours and flatten the layers in your file, so it should be used sparingly and strategically. There may be times when you need to assign a profile, which can affect the way the image looks, but has no permanent effect on the image, unless you convert to another profile after assigning the wrong colour space.

To convert colour profiles, choose Edit, Convert to Profile ... from the menu bar and do the following:

1 Select a Destination Space from the menu.

2 Choose a rendering intent from the menu in the Conversion Options.

3 Leave the Black Point Compensation, Dither and Flatten Image options selected.

4 Click OK.

To assign a colour profile, do the following:

5 Choose Edit, Assign Profile ... from the menu bar.

6 Photoshop will warn you about changing the appearance of layers. Tick the box marked Don't show again (optional) and click OK.

7 Click the circle next to Working RGB or choose a profile from the menu.

8 Optional: try different profiles with the Preview box ticked to see how the colours change. Generally, one will look a lot more correct than the rest.

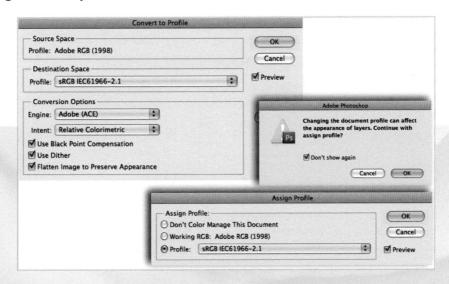

Save an image as a JPEG

There are several ways to create JPEG files in Photoshop. The most direct way is via the File, Save As dialogue. When you save JPEGs in this manner, you can save them at very high resolution.

There are a few considerations when saving JPEG files. The first is image quality. The biggest problem with JPEG files is their characteristic compression artefacts. Be sure to inspect the preview carefully to avoid these issues. JPEG compression can make your files very small by degrading them drastically. Higher-quality images take up more disc space, but even at the highest quality level, lots of data has been discarded. In most cases, JPEG files are going to be used as e-mail attachments or websites, and shown on computer screens, which means you'll typically want to convert the colour profile to sRGB before you make your JPEG. You'll often want to resample the image to a size that fits better on most screens, too (see Chapter 13).

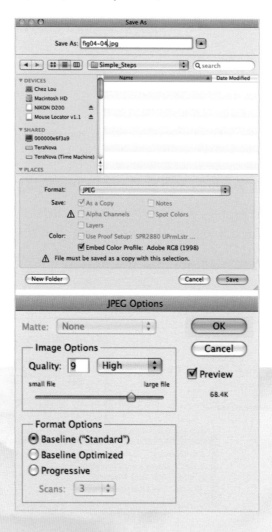

To save as a JPEG, select File, Save As ... from the menu and specify a name and location as with saving PSD files. Then do the following:

1 Select JPEG from the Format menu.

2 Be sure that Embed Color Profile is ticked.

3 Click Save. The JPEG Options dialogue will appear.

4 Set the image quality. Toggle the Preview tick box to see how your settings are affecting the image.

5 Set the Format Options as you like. Progressive files look different as they load.

6 Click OK.

 HOT TIP: If you are familiar with earlier versions of Photoshop, you used to have to convert your 16-bit image to 8-bit mode explicitly before you could save a JPEG. In CS5, you no longer have to.

▶ **SEE ALSO:** Using File, Save As to create a JPEG adds a custom icon consisting of a miniature of the image, which slightly increases the file size. If you are saving a file specifically for the web, the Save for Web & Devices command (see next in this chapter) does not add the icon.

Use Save for Web & Devices

This tool allows you to create images for web pages, e-mail attachments, phones, etc. and save them in any of the main formats that are used on the web, including JPEG and GIF. 2-up and 4-up previews allow you to test your settings before saving, and see what the file size and download time will be.

To use the feature, select File, Save for Web & Devices ... from the menu bar. A dialogue will appear, then do the following:

1 Click the 2-Up tab.

2 Choose JPEG from the File Format menu or select an item from the Preset menu.

3 Tick both Embed Color Profile and Convert to sRGB.

4 Select a level from the Compression Quality menu, enter a number into the Quality field or select Optimize to File Size ... from the Optimize menu and enter a size.

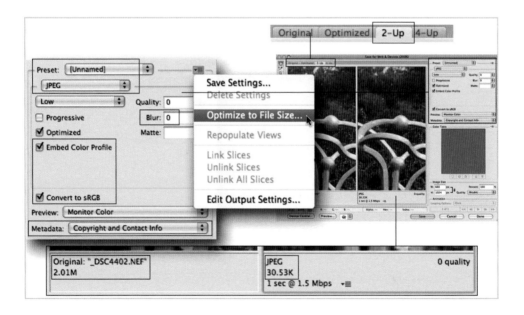

5 Optional: apply blur to reduce artefacts, tick Progressive and/or Optimized as you like.

6 Optional: select the amount of metadata you want to include.

7 Click Save.

8 Enter a name and select a location to save your file.

9 Select Images Only and Default Settings from the Format and Settings menus at the bottom of the dialogue.

10 Click Save.

HOT TIP: Zoom in or out to evaluate the results as you're adjusting your settings. Zooming in to 200% or more will show JPEG artefacts more clearly, but generally you want to evaluate the image at 100%, since that's how other people are most likely to view it.

ALERT: Before using this tool, it's best to resample large images with the Fit Image or Image Size command (see Chapter 13). Save for Web & Devices was designed for preparing smallish images for the web, and you'll get a warning if the file you want to process is too large. If you need to make high-resolution JPEGs, GIFs, etc., use File, Save As ...

DID YOU KNOW? Other features of this dialogue include making animated GIF images, resampling, and slicing images for use in advanced web design. See the help system or the Adobe website for more details.

5 Work with layers and groups

Introduction

Working in layers and pixel-level editing are key capabilities that set Photoshop apart from programs like Apple's Aperture and Adobe's own Lightroom. Layers allow you to composite elements on top of your original to produce a finished result without directly altering the original. This sets the stage for being able to roll back or even store multiple variations of an image in a single file.

Photoshop can create several distinct kinds of layer: Pixel, Adjustment, Fill and Type. Layers can be grouped and they can alter the appearance of the layers beneath them in different ways. They can also be converted into smart objects, which allow you to perform actions like applying filters or scaling the smart object repeatedly without degradation. This chapter will explore ways of working with layers, emphasising best practices and a non-destructive editing process.

Use key elements of the Layers panel

The Layers panel is the central interface for creating and managing layers. Even though there are items in the menu bar that do the same things, the emphasis in this chapter will be on this panel. Almost everything you want to do with layers can be done from there. Hover the mouse pointer over items in the Layer panel for a tooltip explaining what they are.

1 Using the icons at the bottom of the panel, add blank layers, groups and adjustment layers, and then duplicate, link or delete layers, add layer masks, or add layer styles.

2 Select layer-related commands from the menu icon in the upper right corner of the panel.

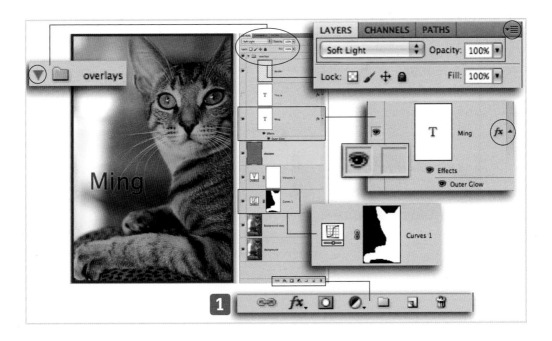

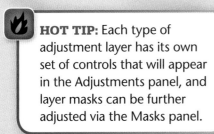

HOT TIP: Each type of adjustment layer has its own set of controls that will appear in the Adjustments panel, and layer masks can be further adjusted via the Masks panel.

3 Click to select a layer and then adjust layer blending mode or opacity with the controls at the top of the panel. Lock pixels, transparency, position or all elements of a layer with the icons just beneath the blending mode menu.

4 Click the eyeball icon to toggle visibility of layers, groups and layer styles.

5 Click the triangle controls to expand or collapse groups.

6 Edit layer masks to control where the effects of adjustment layers are applied in the image.

7 Ctrl-click/right-click on thumbnails, masks and layer names to display different context-sensitive menus.

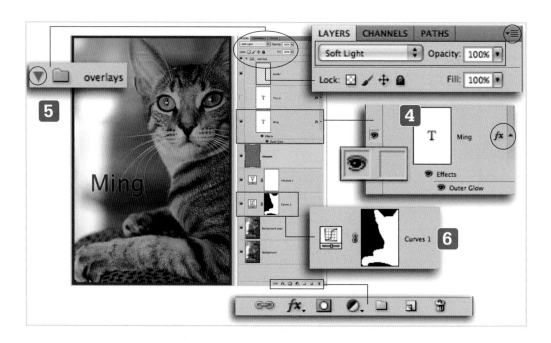

Duplicate a layer

Many tasks in retouching begin with duplicating a layer such as the background. This is a way of creating a kind of internal backup for your file. You can use the eyeball icon to turn off the visibility of the original layer, and then edit the copy. If you don't like the edit, you can delete the copy and reduplicate the original to start over.

To duplicate a layer, do any of the following:

1 Drag the layer to the Create a new layer icon at the bottom of the panel and release the mouse button when the tip of the mouse pointer touches the icon.

2 Click the layer to select it and then use Command/Ctrl + J.

3 Select Layer, New, Layer via Copy from the menu bar.

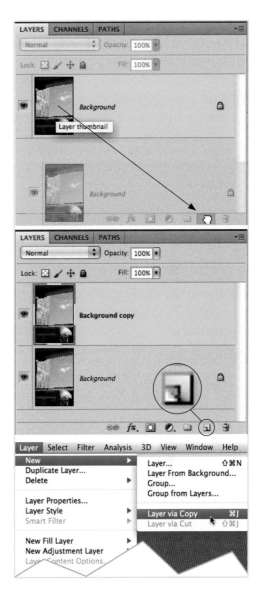

ALERT: If you make a selection in the image before you use Command/Ctrl + J, you will copy the selected area to a new layer. If you don't want that, be sure to deselect with Command/Ctrl + D first.

HOT TIP: Sometimes it is useful to convert the background layer into a conventional layer. Hold down Option/Alt and double-click to convert it to a layer, or just double-click to convert with options.

Make a layer via copy or cut

It is often useful to duplicate part of an image on to another layer and then reposition or transform the duplicate. You can leave the original layer intact or cut the part out of the original layer.

1 Use one of the selection tools to select the part of the image that you want to copy or cut (see Chapter 8 for details).

2 To copy to a new layer, use Command/ Ctrl + J.

3 Use the move tool to reposition the element.

4 To cut to a new layer, use Shift + Command/ Ctrl + J.

5 Optional: use Free Transform (Command/ Ctrl + T) to reposition and reshape the new element.

6 Optional: use a mask or the Eraser tool to make the item fit its new location.

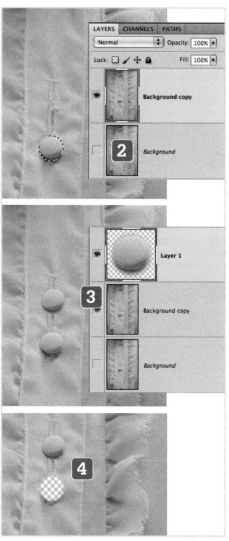

SEE ALSO: It's often a good idea to feather the selection before you copy or cut to a new layer. The edges will blend more easily. See Chapter 8 for details.

Create a blank layer and fill all or part of it

Blank pixel layers are very versatile. They can be used simply to add a block of colour to a region, but they can also be used with tools like the spot healing brush or the mixer brush to apply edits on a separate layer from the original. That makes the edits easily reversible, and you can turn the visibility of the layer on and off to see how your edits are working.

1 Click on a layer to select it.

2 Click the Create a New Layer icon. The new layer will be created above the previously selected layer.

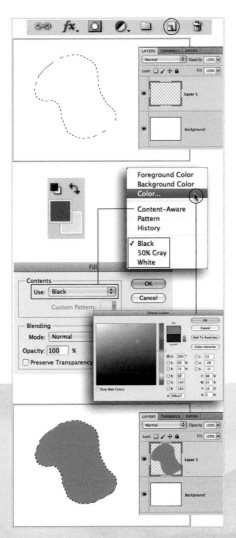

3 Optional: use the Lasso or any selection tool to create a selection (see Chapter 8). If you don't create a selection, the following techniques will fill the entire layer.

To fill the selection or layer, do one of the following:

4 Use Option/Alt + Delete/Backspace to fill with the foreground colour in the Tools panel.

5 Use Command/Ctrl + Delete/Backspace to fill with the background colour.

6 Select Edit, Fill ... from the menu bar then:

- Select a colour from the menu; or
- Select Color... from the menu
- Use the dialogue to select a colour and click OK.

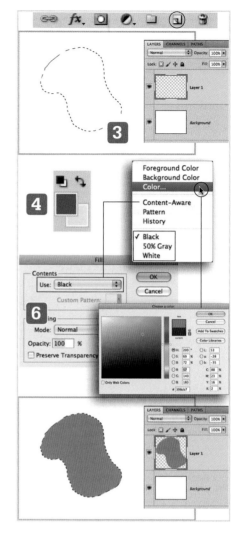

ALERT: After you fill a selection, the selection is still active. Unless you want to perform further actions upon that selection (e.g. adding a stroke or adding a masked adjustment), make sure to deselect (Command/Ctrl + D).

SEE ALSO: The Color Picker dialogue is covered in Chapter 7.

Mix layers with Opacity and Blending modes

When you place two image layers together in Photoshop, the pixels of the layer on top completely obscure the pixels directly beneath them, unless you reduce the Opacity or change the Blending mode of the layer above. Reducing the Opacity setting makes layers more translucent, while Blending modes combine the content of the layers in different ways to produce sometimes dramatic results. If the effect of a particular Blending mode is too strong, you can rein it in by reducing the Opacity of that layer.

You can also set the Blending mode of an adjustment layer, such as a Black and White layer. Using Blending modes with groups can be a little tricky. The layers inside the group will blend as expected, but the group as a whole acts like a layer that is set to another mode. The results can sometimes be unexpected. Unlike layers, the default Blending mode for groups is Pass Through, not Normal.

 HOT TIP: When you use a Blending mode, the top layer determines the appearance of the image – if you reverse the layers and use the same Blending mode, you can get very different results.

The Blending modes are grouped in the menu as follows:

1 Normal and Dissolve: Dissolve only works with layers that have feathered areas.

2 The darkening group (e.g. Color Burn).

3 The lightening group (e.g. Lighten).

4 The contrast group (e.g. Overlay).

5 The comparative group (e.g. Difference).

6 The HSL influencing group (e.g. Hue).

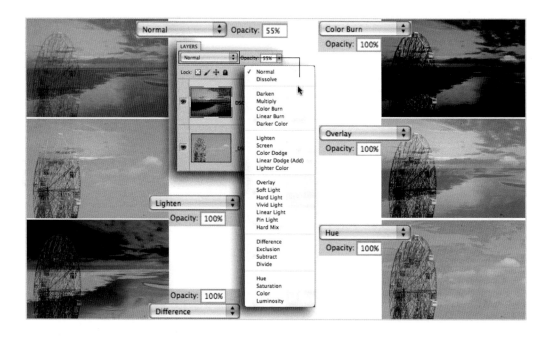

SEE ALSO: When you blend layers by reducing opacity, the result often lacks contrast. You can add a curves adjustment layer to add more 'pop' to the image.

Use Blending Options and reorder layers

The Blending Options dialogue offers sophisticated options for mixing layers in ways that are completely unlike using transparency or Blending Modes. The sliders in the Blend If section determine whether areas of the top layer drop away ('knock out') or parts of the underlying layer punch through, based on either tonality or colour. This is a tool where experimentation pays off.

When blending layers or arranging composites, the stacking order of the layers often makes a difference. Drag layers up or down in the Layers panel to change their order. The dividing line between the layers will double to indicate where the layer will land if you release the mouse button.

To use Blending Options:

1 Select Blending Options ... from the Add a layer style menu (*fx* icon) at the bottom of the Layers panel.

2 To blend based on colour instead of tonality, select one or more channels from the Blend If menu. (Adjust the sliders separately for each channel.)

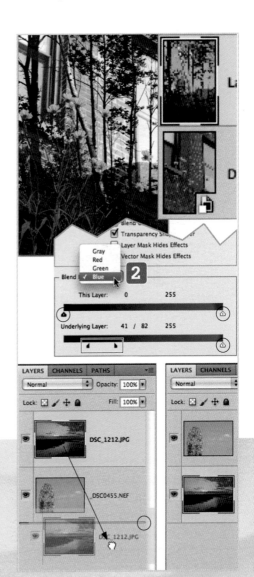

3 Move the sliders in the section marked This Layer to knock out parts of the top image.

4 Move the sliders in the section marked Underlying Layer to make them punch through the top layer.

5 Hold the Option/Alt key and drag either side of the sliders to split them. This feathers the transition of the effect.

6 Adjust General and Advanced blending options as needed.

7 Click OK.

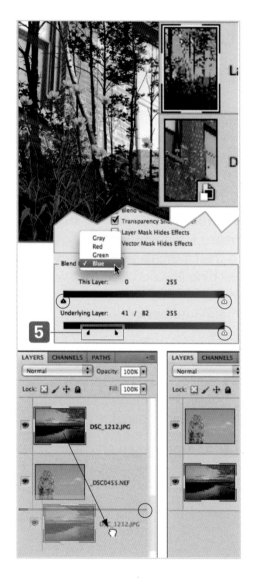

 HOT TIP: You can also use Command/Ctrl + [or] to move layers up and down with the keyboard.

Use layer masks

Layer masks are a core element of a non-destructive editing strategy. Instead of permanently erasing pixels, you can mask a layer. If you discover later that you have removed too much or too little of the layer, you simply edit the mask. On adjustment layers, masks allow pixel-level control of where the effects of an adjustment layer are applied.

In all cases, masks operate by the same principle: a mask is a map of the image where the colour black blocks. The black pixels in the mask hide the corresponding pixels in the layer it is attached to, or they block the effect of adjustment layers, etc. from being applied to those pixels. Grey pixels block more or less, depending on how dark the grey is. Black has a value of zero and white has a value of 255. The grey values range from 1 to 254.

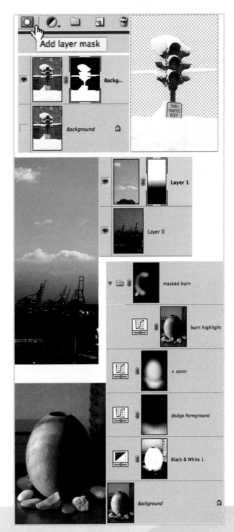

You can add masks to layers and groups. Just click on the layer or group to select it, and then click on the Add layer mask icon at the bottom of the Layers panel. Adjustment layers, Fill layers and smart filters all have layer masks attached when you create them. The Create new fill or Adjustment layer icon is immediately to the right of the Add layer mask icon, and contains a menu of layer types you can add.

If you have a selection of 'marching ants' active when you create any layer that comes with a built-in mask, or you add a layer mask, then the active selection will be converted into the mask for that layer. The black part of the mask will correspond to the parts of the image that were not selected. The rest will become white (or grey – pixels can be partially selected). You can also fill a mask with a solid colour, paint it, apply a gradient, invert it, apply adjustments or run filters on it.

 DID YOU KNOW?

Two areas worth exploring are channels and paths. Whenever you save a mask, it appears in the Channels panel. You can also use the Red, Green or Blue channels as a starting point for advanced masks and selections. Photoshop can create Vector masks, which use paths rather than pixels to define areas. Paths are hard-edged and resolution independent. You create and edit paths with the Pen tool.

Use the Masks panel

You can refine any mask with the Masks panel. The Density and Feather settings in the panel are non-destructive: in other words, you can change or revert those settings as much as you like without degrading the mask.

1 Click on the mask thumbnail to select it. Bracket marks will surround the corners of the thumbnail.

2 Activate the Masks panel. (If you do not see it in the Dock, select Window, Masks from the menu bar.)

3 Use the Density slider to decrease the effect of the mask.

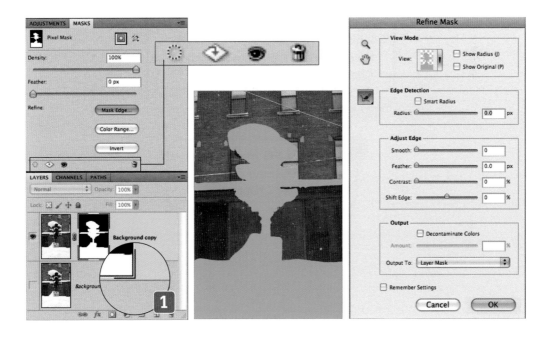

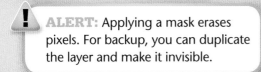

ALERT: Applying a mask erases pixels. For backup, you can duplicate the layer and make it invisible.

4 Use the Feather slider to soften the edges of the mask.

5 Click Mask Edge … to open the Refine Mask dialogue.

6 Click Color Range … to revise the mask by sampling colours.

7 Click Invert to reverse what the mask shows or hides.

8 Click the eyeball icon at the bottom of the panel to disable or enable the mask.

9 Use the other icons to load a selection based on the mask, delete the mask, or apply it to the layer.

▶ **SEE ALSO:** The Quick Selection view in the Refine Edge dialogue looks that way because the settings have been changed from the default. Changing those settings will be discussed later in this chapter.

▶ **SEE ALSO:** For more details on using Color Range, see Chapter 8.

Use the Refine Mask dialogue

This dialogue offers several tools to improve the edges in complex masks. The same dialogue comes up when you want to refine a selection. The Smart Radius feature was designed particularly for images that have a mix of hard and soft edges, and does a good job of extracting hair from a background. The tool won't do the entire job for you, but it will quickly take you a lot further than older techniques did. Selecting, masking and extracting are techniques that come with practice and are generally done with different tools to handle different parts of the task.

To open the dialogue, click the mask thumbnail in the Layers panel, and then click the Mask Edge ... button in the Masks panel or choose Select, Refine Mask... from the menu bar (keyboard shortcut: Option/Alt + Command/Ctrl + R).

1 Tap the F key to cycle through the view modes to find the one that works best for the image you are working on.

2 Optional: activate the Radius (tap J) and Original (tap P) view mode boxes as needed.

3 To use Edge Detection, move the radius slider.

4 Tick the Smart Radius box and increase the radius for images that have a mix of hard and soft edges. The tool works well with very high radius settings.

5 Tap the E key to activate the Refine Radius tool. Paint with the tool (+ mode) to select elements, or hold down the Option/Alt key (− mode) to mask out elements. Use the [and] keys to change the size of the brush.

6 Use the Adjust Edge sliders as needed.

? DID YOU KNOW?

This example began with an easy selection of the background using the Quick Select tool – it's sometimes easier to select the part you don't want and then invert the mask when you're done.

! ALERT: Decontaminate Colors alters the pixels in your image. Because of this, it requires you to make a new layer or document. It is a good idea to keep the original layer (just make it invisible), so that you can revert, if needed.

7 Use the Output section to decontaminate colour fringes and create a new layer. To see how the colours are changing, tap the R key to activate the Reveal Layer view.

8 Click OK to apply the refinements.

9 Optional: click Invert in the Masks panel or use Command/Ctrl + I to finalise the mask.

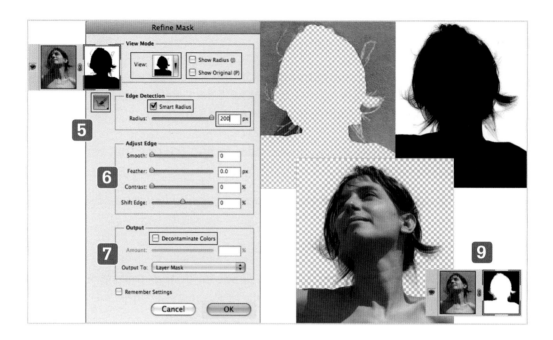

HOT TIP: To extract fine hair from a background, use Smart Radius with a high setting. Painting over fly-away areas with the Refine Edge tool in + mode can clean up edges.

View a mask as an overlay

When working with masks, it is sometimes helpful to see it in context. When you view the mask as an overlay on the image, you can gauge if your mask goes too far over an edge, or doesn't reach far enough. You can click on a layer (or group) and tap the backslash (\) key to display its mask as an overlay, and dialogues such as Refine Edge have options to display your selection as a quick mask overlay.

Photoshop's default setting is to show masks as a 50 per cent red overlay, which can be hard to read. This example will show how to change the Layer Mask Display Options and the Quick Mask Options to something more usable.

1 Double-click a layer mask to open the settings dialogue.

2 Change the Opacity as needed.

3 Click on the colour chip to open the Color Picker dialogue.

4 Select a colour that is not likely to appear in your image, such as fluorescent green (enter 66ff00 into the box marked # at the bottom of the dialogue).

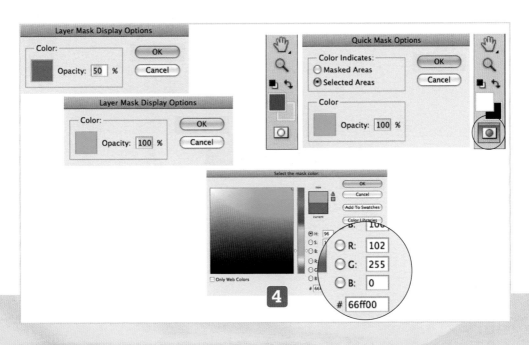

 HOT TIP: 100 per cent opacity generally works well, but there may be times where you need to see through the overlay. You can back the opacity off, and change it again when you need to.

5 Click OK to commit the Color Picker and then click OK to accept the setting.

6 Tap the \ key to toggle the overlay on and off.

Now, to change the Quick Mask settings:

7 Double-click the Quick Mask icon at the bottom of the Tools panel to open the Settings dialogue.

8 Click the circle next to Selected Areas.

9 Change the Opacity and Color settings as in the Layer Mask dialogue and click OK to accept.

10 You are probably still in Quick Mask mode. Click the icon or tap the Q key to exit.

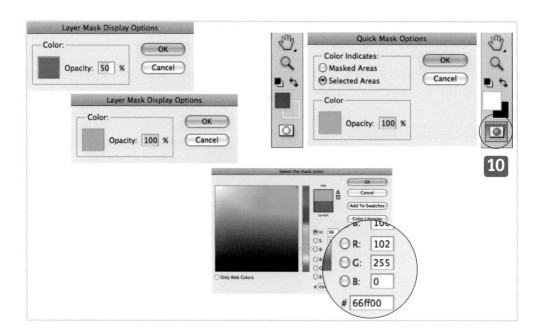

Evaluate and work with a mask directly

Even with Photoshop's automated tools to help you make a mask, you may still find that you need either to build or to refine your mask by hand. When the mask is selected, any tool that you apply in the image window will affect the mask instead of the pixels. Brush tools, copy, paste, fill and filters can all be used.

Aside from viewing a mask as an overlay, you can temporarily disable it to see how it is working. You can also view the mask in the image window to edit it directly. In some cases, you'll want to discard a mask altogether, and in others you'll want to apply the mask and permanently erase the pixels from the layer. Just as masks can be made from selections, you can load selections from masks.

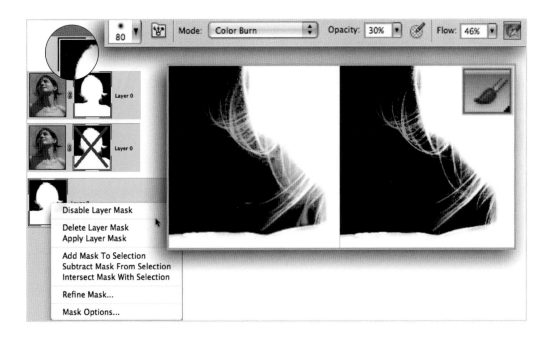

ALERT: It's easy to accidentally paint into your pixels when you want to edit the mask or vice versa. Look for bracket marks around the corners of the mask thumbnail or the layer thumbnail to know which is currently being edited. If you do make a mistake, you can use Undo or the History panel to revert.

1. Shift-click on a mask to enable or disable it. A red X appears through the mask when it is disabled.

2. Click on the mask thumbnail to select the mask for editing.

3. Option/Alt-click on the mask thumbnail to view and modify the mask in the image editing area or return to the normal view.

4. Paint in black or white to edit the mask. Use opacity, fill, brush size, hardness, and blending modes to build tone slowly and constrain how colour is applied.

5. Ctrl-click/right-click on the mask thumbnail to display its menu. Options include deleting or applying the mask.

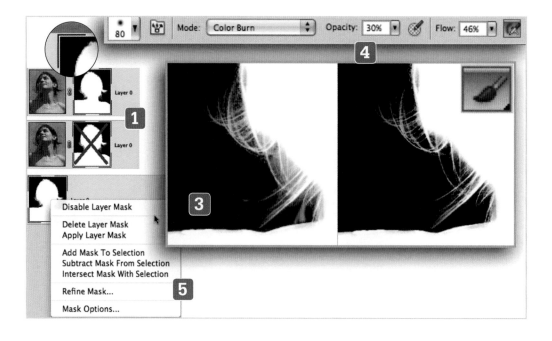

 HOT TIP: You can refine areas of your mask by forcing them to black or white while preserving edges (e.g. to further refine hair extraction). Use a brush with the foreground colour set to white and 50% or lower opacity and the blending mode set to Colour Dodge to force greys to white, or set the foreground colour to black and the blending mode to Color Burn to force greys to black. You can also reduce the flow to slow the application of colour. Don't brush over the same area too many times, or you'll lose the edge.

Select multiple layers

To select multiple layers, click the first layer to select it, then either:

1 For a contiguous selection: Shift-click the second layer to select it and all layers in between.

2 For a discontiguous selection: Command/Ctrl-click on the labels of the additional layers you want to select.

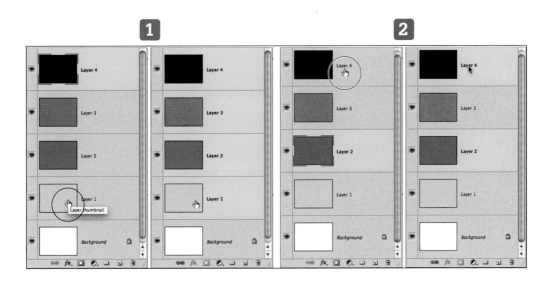

! **ALERT:** If you Command/Ctrl-click on a layer thumbnail or a mask thumbnail, you will load the layer's transparency or load the mask as a selection. You can only make a discontiguous selection in the Layers panel by clicking on the labels.

? **DID YOU KNOW?**

If you activate the Move tool with more than one layer selected, the Options bar contains buttons to align or distribute the selected layers. It is worthwhile becoming familiar with these.

Nudge, shove and select layers with the Move tool

Once you have selected one or more layers, you can reposition them with the Move tool. When compositing elements, you can also set the Move tool to select layers or groups by clicking in the image area.

1 Select at least two layers via the Layers panel as per the previous example.

2 Tap V on the keyboard or click in the Tools panel to activate the Move tool. Check the Options bar to see that Auto-Select is not ticked.

3 Drag in the image area to reposition; or

4 Use the arrow keys to nudge the elements one pixel at a time; or

5 Hold the Shift key down and use the arrow keys to shove the elements in larger jumps.

6 In the Layers panel, click the background layer to deselect the other layers.

7 Tick the Auto-Select box in the Options bar.

8 Click on an item in the image area and note which layer is selected.

9 Shift-click to select additional layers or deselect layers already selected.

10 Drag, nudge or shove the selected elements as in 4 and 5 above.

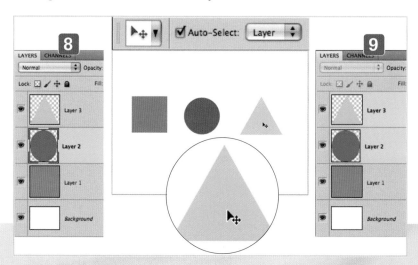

 HOT TIP: Holding down the Command/Ctrl key temporarily converts any tool to the Move tool. When you release the key, the tool reverts to whatever was active. Be careful – it's easy to switch to the Move tool accidentally while using the Brush tool and push your layers out of alignment.

Convert the Background layer

Images normally open in Photoshop with only a locked Background layer. As long as it is locked, you can't move it, mask it or drag layers beneath it.

1 To convert the Background to a normal layer and assign it a name, double-click on it.

2 To bypass the New Layer dialogue, hold down the Option/Alt key and double-click on the Background. Photoshop will unlock the layer and name it Layer 0.

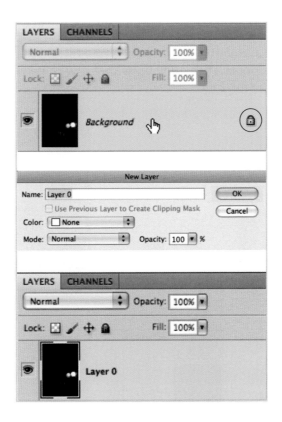

Link layers

Once you have selected several layers (the selection can be discontiguous), you can link them. Once layers are linked, they all move together whenever you nudge any one of them. Whenever you select a linked layer, an indicator will appear on the layers it is linked to.

1 To link layers, select the layers you want to link and then click the link icon at the bottom of the Layers panel.

2 To link additional layers, select any of the linked layers and Command/Ctrl-click the label of the layer(s) you want to add, and then click the link icon again.

3 To unlink layers, select one or more linked layers and then click the link icon. The link indicator will disappear. (Click any layer that it was linked to in order to see that the remaining links are intact.)

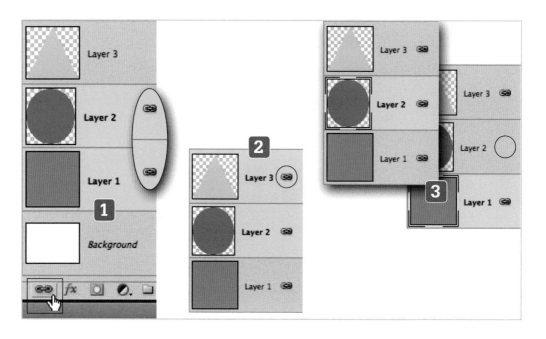

Use groups

One of the easiest ways to create a group is to select the layers first, and invoke a keystroke to place them inside the group in one operation. When you place files into groups, you can move the individual layers independently or select the group and move them together. The same goes for visibility: you can hide individual layers, or hide the entire group in one shot. You can also reduce the opacity of a group. Groups can contain groups nested several levels deep.

1 Select the layers to be included in the group using the methods outlined earlier.

2 Use Command/Ctrl + G or drag the layers to the Create a new group icon at the bottom of the Layers panel.

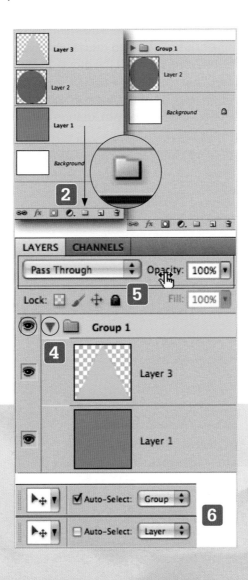

3 Click the eyeball icon to toggle the group's visibility.

4 Click the triangle to expand or collapse the group.

5 Select the group and adjust the opacity setting or the blending mode.

6 Select the group and activate the Move tool (Auto-Select set to Group or unticked) to move all of the layers together.

7 Select a layer within the group and activate the Move tool (Auto-Select set to Layer or unticked) to move an individual layer.

? DID YOU KNOW?

The default blending mode for groups is Pass Through, not Normal. If any of the layers inside your group have a blending mode set, there can be surprising results when you set the blending mode of the group. In some cases, you may find that you need to mask out some parts of the layers in your group, or find a different way to arrange the layers in your file.

! ALERT: If you click the Create a new group icon instead of dragging the layers on to it, a new group will be created, but the layers will not be placed inside it. You can reselect the layers and drag them into the group afterwards, as demonstrated in the next example.

Manage groups: remove or add layers

Just as with reordering layers, you add layers to groups or remove them by dragging them in the Layers panel. The boundary line will double when the layer reaches a drop point.

 To remove layers: expand the group. Drag layers to a drop point outside the group and then release the mouse button.

 To add layers to an expanded group: drag the layer to a drop point at the bottom of the group or to any drop point within the group.

3 To add layers to collapsed groups: drag the layer to the group's folder icon. Release the mouse button when a box surrounds the folder. The layer will land at the bottom of the group.

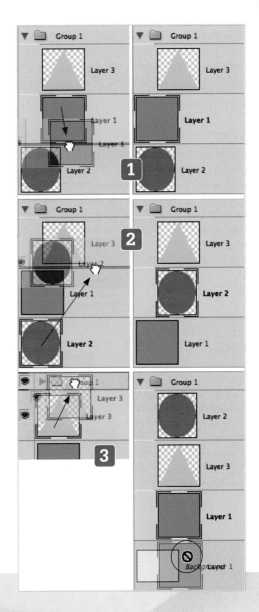

HOT TIP: To remove all layers from a group and discard the group folder, Ctrl-click/right-click on the group's label and choose Ungroup Layers from the menu. (Ctrl-clicking/right-clicking on the folder icon brings up a different menu.)

ALERT: If a group is sitting directly above the background layer, you will not be able to drag layers out of the bottom of the group.

Rename and set styles and properties for layers and groups

To rename a layer or group, simply double-click on its label to go into editing mode. Type the new name and hit Return/Enter to commit the change.

The area that you can double-click to edit the name is actually very precise. If you accidentally double-click outside the label area, you will see either the Layer Style or Group Properties dialogue. Just click Cancel or hit the Esc key, and try again.

When you do want to add a layer style, double-clicking in the area to the right of the label does the same thing as selecting Blending Options ... from the Add a layer style menu at the bottom of the Layers panel.

To colour-code a layer or group, Ctrl-click/right-click on its eyeball icon.

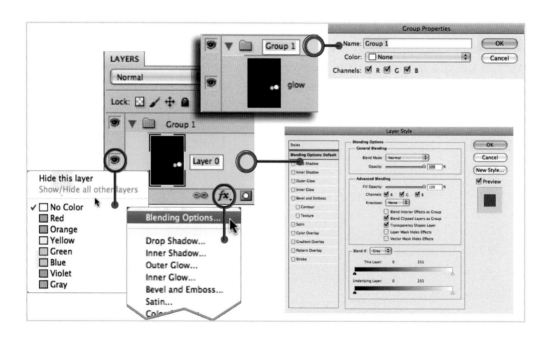

Delete a layer or group

All of the methods listed below will delete one or more layers or groups at the same time. Use the selection methods mentioned earlier to select multiple layers, groups or a mix of both, and then delete using one of these methods:

1 Hit the Delete/Backspace key to delete the item(s) immediately.

2 Drag the item(s) to the dustbin icon at the bottom of the Layers panel to delete immediately.

3 Click the dustbin icon at the bottom of the Layers panel. If you see a confirmation dialogue, click Yes.

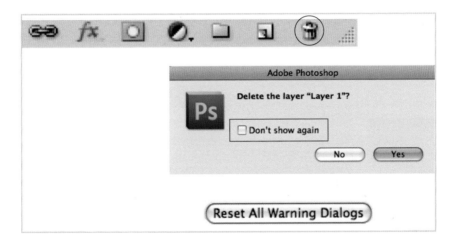

 HOT TIP: The default behaviour for clicking the dustbin icon is to get a message confirming that you want to delete the items. You can tick the box marked Don't show again to avoid these messages in the future.

If you turn off the warning and later decide you want it back, select Photoshop, Preferences, General (Windows: Edit, Preferences, General) from the menu bar, click on Reset All Warning Dialogs at the bottom of the window, and then click OK.

Toggle layer visibility and use layer comps

Hiding and showing layers is a very useful way of evaluating your work. You can toggle an individual layer on and off to see if there is more to do – tweaking a curve, or masking an edge, for example. In some cases, you will want to turn off several layers or evaluate different combinations of layers. You can use the Layer Comps panel to record those combinations, and then easily switch between them.

1 To isolate a layer, Option/Alt-click on the eyeball icon of the layer you want to see. All other layers will be hidden. Option/Alt-click on the same eyeball again to show the other layers again.

2 To hide or show a group of layers, hold the mouse button down to toggle the first eyeball and drag across several others. All of the layers will switch on or off to match the state of the first eyeball.

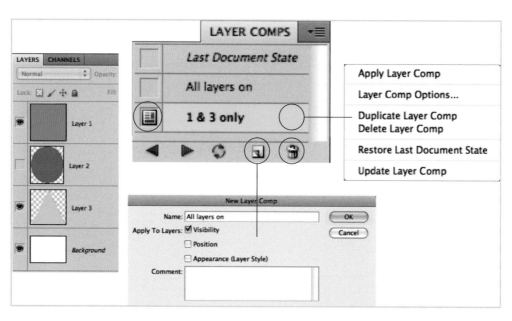

3 Click the Create a new layer comp icon and enter a name. By default, the comp will record the visibility of the layers.

4 Set the position and layer style options or enter a comment as needed.

5 Click OK to save the comp.

6 To apply a layer comp, click the box to the left of its label.

7 To edit the definition of the layer comp, Ctrl-click/right-click on its label and choose Layer Comp Options ...

8 To delete a layer comp, click on it and then click the dustbin icon at the bottom of the panel.

ALERT: When you Option/Alt-click to isolate a layer, be sure to Option/Alt-click again to restore the layers' visibility before you add or delete layers. Otherwise, Photoshop won't remember how to restore the visibility of the other layers.

HOT TIP: If you delete or merge layers, your existing layer comps can get scrambled. In some cases, you can fix them by Ctrl-clicking/right-clicking on the label of each comp and selecting Update Layer Comp from the menu. In other cases, it's best just to delete the comps and redo them.

Merge layers and flatten files

The flexibility of building your file in layers comes at a cost: the size of your file can bloat and affect performance. Print jobs can sometimes go faster if you temporarily flatten your file before starting the job. If you embed a smart object into your file and then edit that smart object, you will have to flatten it before you can resave the edited version.

You can save a flattened copy alongside your master file by simply adding a descriptor to the end of the file name (e.g. image3250.psd and image3250_flat.psd), and then work mainly with the flattened version.

Instead of completely flattening your file, you can merge related groups of layers to reduce the number of layers but still maintain some ability to roll back your file selectively, if you discover problems later.

1 To merge: select two or more layers and choose Layer, Merge Layers (Command/ Ctrl + E) from the menu bar.

2 To merge down: select a layer and use Command/Ctrl + E to merge it with the layer immediately beneath.

3 To flatten: choose Layer, Flatten Image from the menu bar.

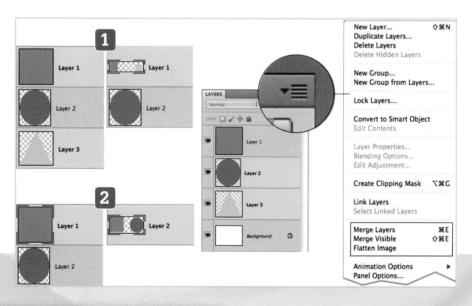

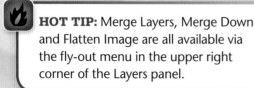

HOT TIP: Merge Layers, Merge Down and Flatten Image are all available via the fly-out menu in the upper right corner of the Layers panel.

Stamp a layer

Stamping a layer effectively fills the selected layer with a flattened copy of your file. This is particularly useful for applying filters, such as smart sharpening, to your project.

1 Select the topmost layer in your file and click the Add a new layer icon.

2 Rename the new blank layer as needed.

3 While holding the Option/Alt key, select Merge Visible from the menu in the upper right corner of the Layers panel.

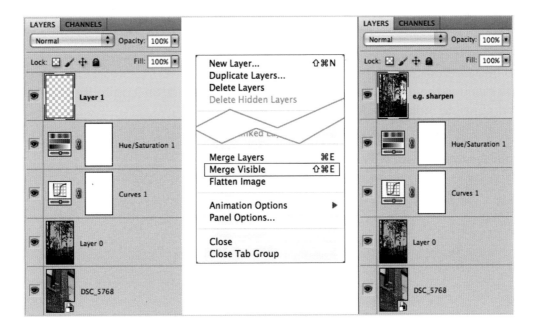

 ALERT: Unless you blend your stamped layer with those beneath, it covers up all the layers below. If you need to change anything in the image, turn off or delete the stamped layer, make your adjustments and then stamp a new layer.

HOT TIP: If your layers flattened, it's because you released the Option/Alt key too soon. Undo and try again.

Convert layers to or from Smart Objects

Smart Objects offer an automatic approach to non-destructive editing. Normally, when you scale, transform or apply a filter to a layer, its pixels are permanently altered, and each successive filter or transformation will further degrade the layer. Smart Objects address the problem by embedding an original copy of the layer. You can scale a Smart Object or apply filters repeatedly without degradation, because Photoshop is working from a fresh copy of the original layer each time.

Smart Objects can make your files very large, so you may want to convert them back to conventional layers once you are satisfied with any transformations or filters that you have applied.

1 To make a Smart Object: select a layer and choose Convert to Smart Object from the menu at the top of the Layers panel. Photoshop adds an icon to the layer thumbnail to indicate that it is a Smart Object.

2 To convert a Smart Object to a conventional layer: select the Smart Object and choose Layer, Rasterize, Smart Object.

DSC_5768

? DID YOU KNOW?

There is a lot more to Smart Objects and non-destructive editing than can be covered here. Consult the Photoshop help system for additional details. Just type 'Smart Object' into the search box.

Edit a Smart Object, use a Smart Filter

Applying filters to Smart Objects is straightforward. You can apply multiple filters to the object, and then readjust the filter or turn it on and off. Photoshop will re-render the result on the fly. Smart Filters also come with a built-in mask, so you can block off areas where you don't want the filter to be applied.

There are some twists to editing and duplicating Smart Objects. When you duplicate a Smart Object with Command/Ctrl + J or via the Create a new layer icon in the Layers panel, the new Smart Object is a clone of the first, and both draw from the same source data. If you edit either one, they will both update.

A separate Copy command allows you to make a new Smart Object from the first with its own source data. Smart Objects created in this way can be edited independently. Choose Layer, Smart Objects, New Smart Object via Copy.

To edit a Smart Object:

1 Double-click on the Smart Object in the Layers panel or select it and choose Edit Contents from the menu in the upper right corner of the Layers panel.

2 Photoshop will show a message indicating that the file you are about to edit has to be flattened before saving and saved in the same location. (You have the option to tick Don't show again.)

3 The file appears in its own editing window. Make your changes, save the flattened file, and close the window. The Smart Object will update in your main Photoshop file.

To apply a Smart Filter:

4 Click on the Smart Object and apply one or more filters (e.g. Filter, Artistic, Cutout).

5 Double-click the filter label to readjust the filter as needed.

6 Double-click the icon at the right edge of the filter to adjust its blending mode.

7 Click on the mask thumbnail and paint with black in the image area to block the Smart Filter effect.

8 Use the eyeball icons to toggle any or all Smart Filters.

9 Shift-click the mask to disable or enable it.

 HOT TIP: When you apply more than one filter to a Smart Object, you can drag the items in the filter list to change the order that the effects are applied. In some cases, this can alter the final image dramatically.

6 View, zoom and navigate

Introduction

An array of viewing tools allows you to quickly unclutter your screen, work at different magnifications, and move around the image easily, even when working at high magnification. The techniques shown here are demonstrated with the windows in Application Frame mode, but they also work with your windows set to the Application Bar mode.

A graphics library called OpenGL enhances many of the tools described in this chapter. OpenGL is built into the graphics card, and if your computer has an older graphics card, it may not be available. To confirm whether your computer supports OpenGL, select Photoshop, Preferences, Performance (Windows: Edit, Preferences, Performance) from the menu bar and look at the GPU Settings section. If you are unable to tick the box marked Enable OpenGL Drawing, your video card does not support it.

Use the Application Frame

The Application Frame presents the entire Photoshop environment inside a unified window, with all of the panels and interface elements docked around the image editing area. One benefit of this arrangement is that even in the Standard screen mode, you can't accidentally click over the edge of your image and switch into another application the way you can with the default Photoshop environment. Best of all, the Application Frame is flexible – you can still detach elements or re-anchor them to the frame as needed.

A tick appears in the menu when the Application Frame is active (choose Window, Application Frame from the menu bar). Most of the illustrations in this book will be displaying the Application Frame. Key elements of the feature are shown in the illustration.

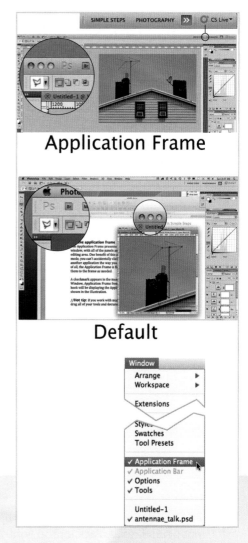

Application Frame

Default

HOT TIP: If you work with multiple monitors, the Application Frame allows you to drag all of your tools and documents between monitors in one shot.

Switch screen modes

No matter how large your display is, working in Photoshop entails dealing with available screen real estate. Photoshop has three screen modes (Standard, Full Screen With Menu and Full Screen) that give increasingly more space to the image. In Standard mode, the image is locked in place, but in either of the Full Screen modes, you can hold down the space bar to drag the image around the viewing area. In Full Screen mode, the panels are hidden along with the menu.

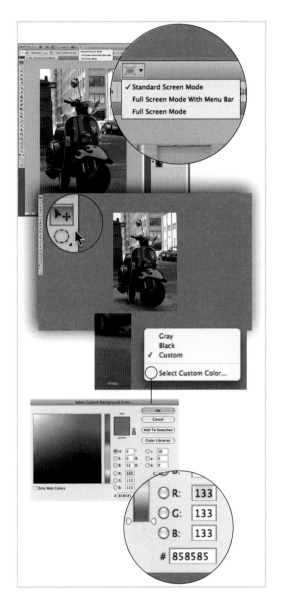

1 Tap the F key repeatedly to cycle through the screen modes.

2 Select a screen mode from the menu at the top of the Photoshop window.

3 Tap the Tab key to show or hide all panels, regardless of screen mode.

4 When the panels are hidden, hover the mouse pointer over the left, right or bottom edge of the screen to reveal a panel. It will snap back when you move the cursor away.

 HOT TIP: Viewing your photo against a background that is not neutral, solid black, or too light will bias your colour and tonal adjustments. Ctrl-click/right-click on the background of the display area and choose Gray from the menu or set a custom colour. To be neutral, your custom colour should have matching Red, Green and Blue values (e.g. 133, 133, 133).

Arrange multiple documents on screen

Depending upon memory and clock speed, you can have several documents open at once. Image windows can be arranged in numerous ways, similar to what you saw with panels earlier. By default, open files are displayed tabs in the image viewing area, with one image visible. Click a tab or select the image name from the Window menu to view the image. The list below shows some options for organising and viewing multiple images.

1 Choose an ordering from the Arrange documents menu at the top of the Photoshop window.

2 Drag tabs within a group to rearrange them. The other tabs will slide apart to show where the tab will appear if you release the mouse button.

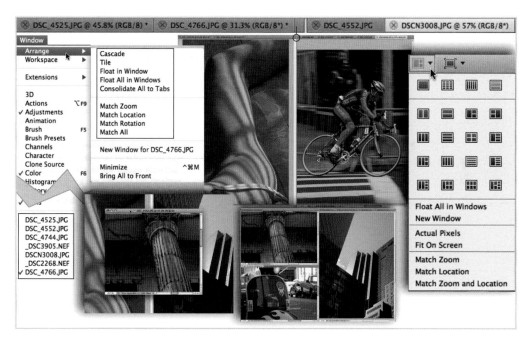

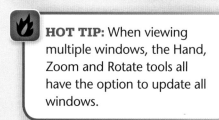

HOT TIP: When viewing multiple windows, the Hand, Zoom and Rotate tools all have the option to update all windows.

3 Drag tabs to the edges of the viewing area to split windows. The tab becomes translucent and a blue line appears to indicate where the tab will snap into place.

4 Drag tabs between groups. The header area of the tab group will turn blue to indicate that the tab will snap into it.

5 Drag tabs downward to tear them free or choose Window, Arrange, Float in Window from the menu bar.

6 Use the Window, Arrange menu to organise windows or match Zoom, Location or Rotation for easy comparison.

Rotate and reset the view

When you draw on paper, you often rotate the paper to make it easier to draw straight lines or move your wrist in a comfortable arc. The Rotate View tool temporarily displays your work at any angle so that you can do the same on screen. Unlike the Image Rotation command (which alters the pixels in your image), Rotate View uses the display card in your computer to present your work at different angles. If you hold the shortcut key instead of tapping it, Photoshop will reactivate the previous tool after you finish rotating the view.

1. Hold the R key to invoke Rotate View. Keep holding the key until you are done. The cursor will change shape and the Options bar will update.

2. Drag in a clockwise or anti-clockwise direction to rotate the view.

3. Release the mouse button and the R key to resume working with the previous tool.

4. To reset the view, hold the R key, click on Reset View in the Options bar, and then release the R key.

 HOT TIP: If your computer has an older graphics display card, the Rotate View tool may not be available.

? DID YOU KNOW?

The menu command Image, Image Rotation is very different from the Rotate View tool. Using Image Rotation repeatedly, especially at arbitrary angles, can degrade your image, because it is recalculating and changing the pixels in your image each time.

Zoom in or out

A new feature of Photoshop CS5 is the Scrubby Zoom option in the Zoom tool, which allows you to increase or decrease magnification arbitrarily by dragging to the right (zoom in) or the left (zoom out). There are also several keystrokes and other tools to adjust magnification. When you zoom in to more than 500 per cent, a grid appears to show individual pixels. You have the option to turn this feature off.

Tap the Z key to switch to the Zoom tool or hold the Z key to use the Zoom tool and revert to the previous tool when you release the key. A number of zooming techniques are listed below.

1. To zoom to a specific percentage: enter a value in the size box at the lower left corner of the image and hit Return/Enter.

2. Use the Zoom Level object at the top of the Photoshop window: select between 25 per cent and 200 per cent from the menu or enter a value into the box and hit Return/Enter.

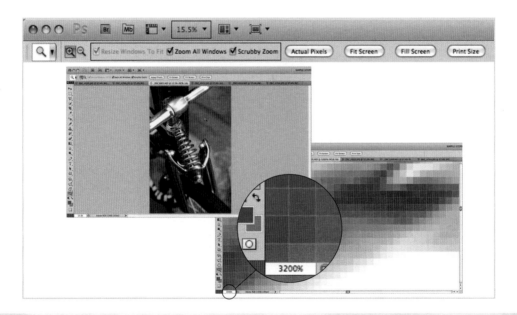

HOT TIP: The pixel grid is an OpenGL feature.

3   Use Command/Ctrl + + (the plus sign) or Command/Ctrl + − (the minus sign) to zoom in or out.

4   Use Command/Ctrl + 0 (zero) or double-click the Hand tool to fit the image in the window.

5   Use Shift + Command/Ctrl + 0 (zero) or double-click the Zoom tool to zoom in to 100 per cent.

6   Use the buttons in the Options bar to set the Zoom level. Actual pixels = 100%.

7   To toggle the pixel grid, select View, Show, Pixel Grid. A tick appears in the menu when the feature is active.

Use the hand tool and Bird's Eye View

At higher levels of magnification (you can zoom in to as much as 3200%), you can literally edit pixel-by-pixel, but only a tiny portion of the image will fit on-screen at one time. You can use the Hand tool to reposition in small increments, Flick Pan to jump in larger increments, or Bird's Eye View to move much larger distances quickly.

1 Hold the space bar to engage the Hand tool temporarily or tap the H key to switch to the tool.

2 Drag in the image with the Hand tool to reposition

3 To use Flick Pan: hold down the mouse button, drag rapidly in a tossing gesture, and release the mouse button. You can click the mouse to catch the image when it scrolls into position, or let it stop on its own.

4 To use Bird's Eye View: hold down the H key and then hold down the mouse button. The image will zoom out. Drag the rectangular outline to a new location and then release the mouse button. The image will zoom back in to the new location. Release the H key to revert to the previous tool.

! **ALERT:** Bird's Eye View and Flick Pan are not available on computers with older graphics cards that do not support OpenGL.

? **DID YOU KNOW?**
Bird's Eye View is an OpenGL feature. If it does not work on your computer, the Navigator panel offers some of that functionality.

Show rulers and grid

You can show rulers when you need to do precision work. The rulers can be set to several different measurement scales. Rulers can be used in conjunction with grids, guides and Snap. Those features will all be discussed shortly.

1. To show rulers, use Command/Ctrl + R or select View, Rulers from the menu bar.

2. To change the ruler scale, Ctrl-click/right-click on one of the rulers and select a new scale from the menu.

3. To toggle the grid display, select Show Grids from the View Extras menu at the top of the Photoshop window or View, Show, Grid from the menu bar.

Use guides

Guidelines can be used to align things visually. You can drag guides into place, or specify a precise location. Photoshop can also show Smart Guides that automatically indicate alignment of edges, midpoints, etc.

1 Hold the mouse button down on one of the rulers and drag to drop guides on to your image.

2 Select the Move tool and drag guides to reposition them once they have been added.

3 Select View, New Guide ... from the menu bar to place guides in precise locations. Just enter a number to use the ruler's current unit of measurement, or add an abbreviation such as cm to specify a different scale.

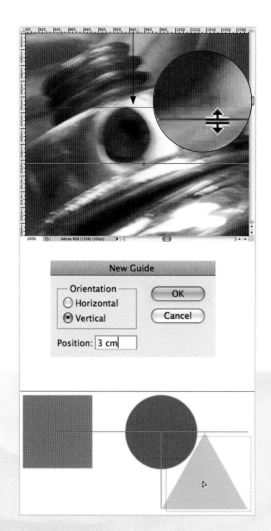

4 Use the View Extras menu at the top of the Photoshop window and select Show Guides to toggle just the guides.

5 Select View, Show, Smart Guides to toggle Smart Guides.

6 Select View, Extras from the menu (Command/Ctrl + H) to hide or reveal guides and all other Extras.

7 Drag guides back to the ruler to remove individual guides.

8 Select View, Clear Guides to clear all guides.

9 Choose View, Lock Guides from the menu bar to lock or unlock guides. A tick will appear next to the item when the guides are locked.

 HOT TIP: Use %, pica and the following abbreviations to specify units in the New Guide dialogue: px: pixels; cm: centimetres; mm: millimetres; pt: points; in: inches.

 ALERT: For the most accurate placement of guides, view the image at 100% or use the Info panel.

Change guide and grid colours and grid divisions

The default colours for guides and the grid can be hard to see, but it's easy to change them. You define the grid divisions in the same dialogue that you use to set the grid and guide colours.

1 Select Photoshop, Preferences, Guides, Grid & Slices (Windows: Edit, Preferences, Guides, Grid & Slices) to open that page of the Preferences dialogue.

2 Select pre-defined colours from the menus or click on the colour chips for any items to select a custom colour (e.g. #3866f4 for guides) via the Color Picker dialogue. Click OK to accept the colour.

3 Enter Gridline Spacing, Scale and Subdivisions as needed.

4 Optional: change the line style for grids and/or guides.

5 Click OK.

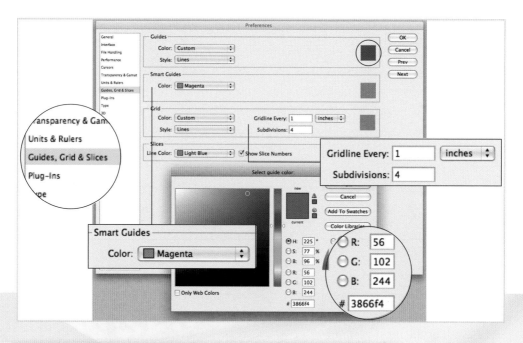

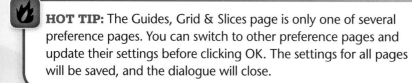

HOT TIP: The Guides, Grid & Slices page is only one of several preference pages. You can switch to other preference pages and update their settings before clicking OK. The settings for all pages will be saved, and the dialogue will close.

Use Snap

With Snap turned on, the Brush, Marquee and other tools will gravitate towards guides or gridlines, which can make some drawing, painting and positioning tasks much simpler. At other times, Snap can thwart your intention to place something at a precise point. You can toggle Snap from the menu bar or via a keystroke.

1 Select View, Snap from the menu bar to toggle. A tick appears in the menu to indicate that Snap is active.

2 Use the View, Snap To menu to specify which objects will snap.

3 With Snap active, it is easy to paint in straight lines along guides or gridlines.

4 Place guidelines and use Snap to make precise selections with the Marquee tool.

5 Use the Marquee tool to make a selection, activate Snap, and drag guidelines until they snap on to the selection.

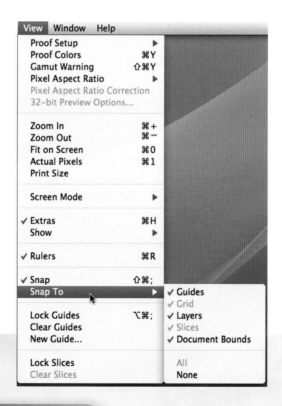

 HOT TIP: Use Shift + Command/Ctrl + ; (semicolon) to toggle Snap via the keyboard.

Hide or show Extras

Guides, grids and 'marching ant' selections are examples of Extras – these items help you edit your image, but do not appear in prints or exported files. You can switch Extras on or off individually or as a group, and you can see which ones are enabled by selecting View, Show, Extras from the menu bar. Active Extras have a tick next to them.

1️⃣ Use the View Extras menu at the top of the Photoshop window to toggle guides, grids and rulers.

2️⃣ To enable and show or disable an individual Extra, select View, Show, Extras, [Extra name] from the menu.

3️⃣ To show or hide all Extras, select View, Extras (Command/Ctrl + H) from the menu bar.

4️⃣ Enable or disable all Extras by selecting View, Show, All or View, Show, None from the menu bar.

5️⃣ Select View, Show, Show Extras Options … to enable or disable multiple Extras in one shot.

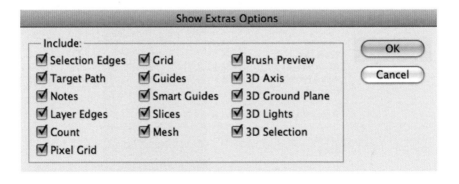

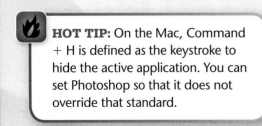

HOT TIP: On the Mac, Command + H is defined as the keystroke to hide the active application. You can set Photoshop so that it does not override that standard.

7 Paint and work with Brush tools

Introduction

Many tools in Photoshop, such as the Clone Stamp, the Healing Brush and the Eraser tool are based on the Brush tool's engine. Once you activate a brush-based tool, you can affect its behaviour through three related panels: the Brush panel, the Brush Presets panel and the Tool Presets panel. In this chapter, we'll explore the characteristics of some of the brush-based tools.

The tools that are powered by Photoshop's brush engine are grouped under six different buttons in the Tools panel as follows:

- Brush tool, Pencil tool, Color Replacement tool and Mixer Brush
- Clone Stamp and Pattern Stamp
- History brush and Art History brush
- Eraser, Background Eraser and Magic Eraser
- Blur, Sharpen and Smudge tools
- Dodge, Burn and Sponge tools

Activate a Brush tool and use the Options bar

The controls for the brush-based tools all work in a similar fashion, with some variations as to which options are available. In this example, we'll use the Brush tool.

To activate the Brush tool, do one of the following:

1 Tap the letter B on your keyboard.

2 Tap Shift + B to rotate through the related tools in the button until the Brush tool is activated.

3 Hold the mouse button down on the Brush tool button and select the tool from the fly-out menu.

Use the Options bar to do any of the following:

4 Select an item from the Tool Preset menu.

5 Select from the Brush Presets menu and set size and hardness.

6 Click the icon to open the Brush panel.

7 Set the blending mode of the brush.

8 Adjust the Opacity of the brush.

9 Activate the Airbrush mode and adjust the Flow.

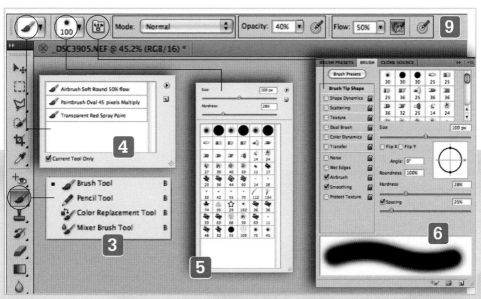

Use Brush presets

Brush presets record the shape and hardness of the current brush, along with its size (optional) and any Brush panel settings, such as shape dynamics or noise. Whenever you activate a brush-based tool, a button for the Brush Preset Picker will appear in the Options bar. Click the button to open the Preset Picker.

1 Select from the panel menu to change the style of preview (e.g. stroke thumbnail) and manage presets.

2 Hover the mouse pointer over a preview for a tooltip showing more information.

3 Click on a preview to activate that brush tip.

4 Adjust size or hardness and click the New Preset icon to add one.

5 Hit the Return/Enter key to dismiss the Brush Presets dialogue.

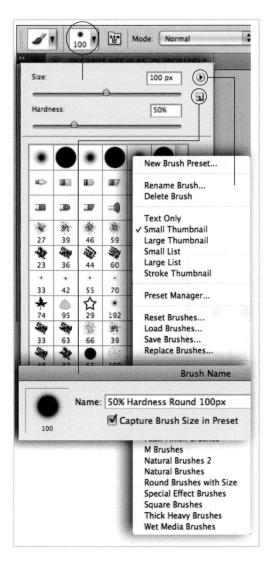

 HOT TIP: When you add a new preset, it is placed at the end of the presets list. Use the Preset Picker's menu to open the Preset Manager and rearrange your presets.

 DID YOU KNOW?
Brush tips are stored in libraries that appear at the bottom of the menu in the upper right corner of the Preset Picker. When you select one of these libraries, you can append the brush tips or replace the current list. You can also save your own libraries and reset the list to the defaults.

Use default colours or select foreground and background colours

The default colours are black foreground/white background for pixel layers and white foreground/black background for masks. You can also select foreground colours from the Swatches panel or use the Color Picker dialogue to select foreground or background colours.

1 To use the default colours, tap D or click on the default colours icon in the Tools panel.

2 Tap X or click on the bent arrow icon in the Tools panel to swap foreground and background colours.

3 To select a colour for the foreground or background, click on the foreground or background colour chip to use the Color Picker dialogue.

4 Open the Swatches panel (Window, Swatches from the menu) and click on a colour chip to set the foreground colour. Hover the cursor over a colour chip to see its name.

To use the Color Picker:

5 Click or drag in the vertical strip to select a hue, and then click in the box on the left to select a tone, tint or shade, or

6 Enter an RGB, web hex, CMYK, Lab or HSB value to specify a colour; or

7 Click Color Libraries to select a Pantone colour. Click to select a colour or type the Pantone number to jump to it in the list. Click the Picker button to return to the main dialogue.

 HOT TIP: You can always add the current foreground colour to your swatches. Open the Swatches panel and click the new swatch icon. Double-click a swatch to rename it. To delete a swatch, drag it to the dustbin icon in the Swatches panel.

8 Optional: click Add To Swatches for easy access to the colour in the future.

9 Click OK to close the dialogue.

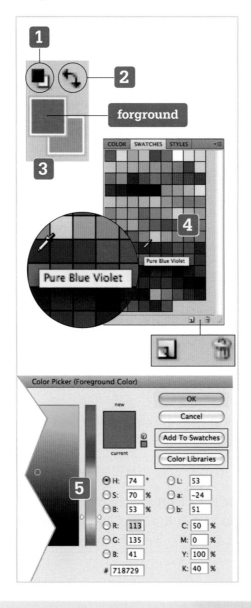

Sample colour from the image

The Eyedropper tool allows you to sample colours from your image. When you activate the Eyedropper tool from the Tools panel, you can set operating parameters for it. Once the Eyedropper is set up, you can convert any brush tool to the Eyedropper tool on the fly, and those parameters will apply.

1 Click in the Tools panel to activate the Eyedropper tool.

2 In the Options bar, set Sample Size to 3 by 3 Average (recommended) or Point Sample, set Sample to All Layers, and tick Show Sampling Ring.

3 Click in the image to sample. The top half of the ring shows the new colour and the bottom half shows the previous foreground colour.

4 With a brush-based tool active: Option/Alt-click in the image to sample with the Eyedropper tool and continue painting.

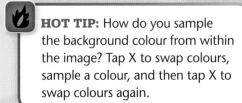

ALERT: The colour ring on the Eyedropper tool is an OpenGL feature.

HOT TIP: How do you sample the background colour from within the image? Tap X to swap colours, sample a colour, and then tap X to swap colours again.

Use the HUD Color Picker

The HUD (heads up display) Color Picker is an alternative to the Color Picker dialogue shown in the previous example. It lets you choose colours in the context of the image.

To set the style of HUD Color Picker, choose Photoshop, Preferences, General from the menu bar and choose one of the Hue Wheel or Hue Strip options from the HUD Color picker menu.

To use the HUD Color Picker:

1 Activate a brush tool.

2 Hold down Ctrl + Option + Command and then click in the image (Windows: Shift + Alt + right-click). The HUD Picker will appear.

3 Keep holding the mouse button down, but release the other keys.

4 Move the mouse to select a hue from the colour wheel or strip.

5 Hold the space bar to lock your hue selection, move the mouse pointer to the saturation/tint/shade box, and then release the space bar.

6 Choose a tone, tint or shade from the box.

7 Release the mouse button to exit the HUD Color Picker.

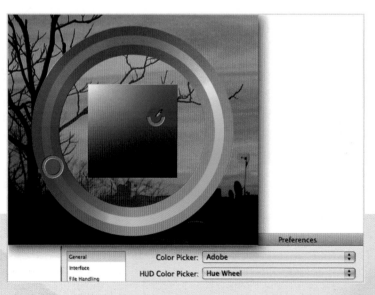

! ALERT: The HUD Color Picker is an OpenGL feature.

Change brush parameters with less effort

Photoshop has a number of ways to reduce the number of times you have to drag your mouse from one side of the screen to the other and back, just to change a setting. Photoshop's keyboard shortcuts are helpful, and now CS5 allows you to change the hardness and the size of the brush by simply dragging.

1 Hold down Ctrl + Option (Windows: Alt + right-click) and drag right or left to increase or decrease the size of the brush respectively. A preview will indicate brush size.

2 Hold down Ctrl + Option (Windows: Alt + right-click) and drag up or down to decrease or increase the hardness of the brush respectively. A preview will indicate brush hardness.

3 Tap the [or] (square bracket) key to decrease or increase the size of the brush respectively.

4 Hold the Shift key down and tap the [or] (square bracket) key to respectively decrease or increase the size of the brush in 25 per cent steps.

5 When the Airbrush mode is active, tap the 1 through 9 keys to set the Flow to 10 per cent to 90 per cent respectively. Tap 0 to set the flow to 100 per cent. Hold the Shift key down to change Opacity with the same shortcuts.

6 When the Airbrush mode is off, tap 0–9 to change Opacity.

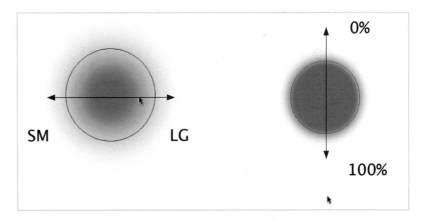

DID YOU KNOW?

When a graphics tablet is attached, two toggle buttons in the Options bar allow you to use stylus pressure to control Opacity and Size, overriding any Brush panel settings. Painting with a stylus is much more like working with an actual brush. Other Brush panel controls can be set to respond to pen pressure, tilt and even barrel rotation, depending on the model of tablet you use. Two popular models are the Bamboo and Intuous4 from Wacom.

Use a Brush tool with opacity

You can build up colour slowly by using a brush-based tool at low opacity. This is especially useful for working with masks. The Opacity setting determines the maximum density of colour applied in one brush stroke, but you can release the mouse button and stroke over the area again to increase density.

1 Select a brush-based tool.

2 Set Opacity in the Options bar.

3 For blended edges, set the brush hardness to a low value.

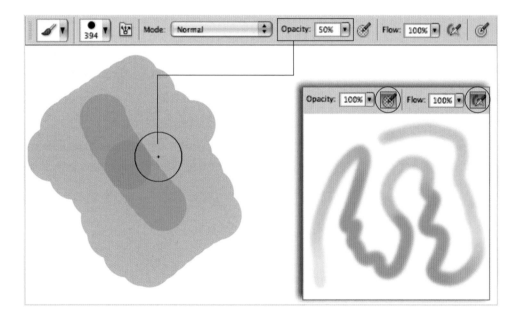

? DID YOU KNOW?

The inset image shows one continuous mark made by an airbrush with Opacity set to pen pressure control.

Use Airbrush mode

As long as you hold the mouse button down, the Airbrush will apply increasingly more colour to your image until it reaches 100 per cent opacity.

The Flow setting controls the speed of the build-up. With a low flow, the Airbrush effects look like low opacity, but there is a difference: if you hold the brush in one place or go back over an area without releasing the mouse button, the colour will continue to build. If the hardness is low, the colour will also slowly bleed out beyond the boundary of the brush.

When you also use the Opacity setting, it controls how much density can be applied in one stroke. Using low flow and low opacity together allows you to build smooth and subtle transitions of tone.

1 Airbrush, 50 per cent flow, 100 per cent opacity: stroke to the right, then hold in place before releasing the mouse button.

2 Airbrush, 50 per cent flow, 40 per cent opacity with overlapping strokes.

? DID YOU KNOW?

Beyond the two pressure controls in the Options bar, there are a number of settings in the Brush panel that can be controlled by a graphics tablet.

Use the Mixer Brush

The Mixer Brush tool is also new in Photoshop CS5. It emulates natural media by allowing you to treat an image as if it's wet paint. You can use any brush tip with the Mixer Brush, but the bristle tips are a perfect match.

The Mixer Brush has a Sample All Layers option, which allows you to use the brush non-destructively by painting on to an empty layer. That means you can erase and redo parts of it, blend it, turn it off or delete the layer, as you choose. You can load the brush with colours from within the image or from another image, or you can select colours using a colour picker or swatches. The Wetness and Mix settings will determine how the colours on the brush blend into the image.

1 Add an empty layer at the top of your image.

2 Activate the Mixer Brush in the Tools panel.

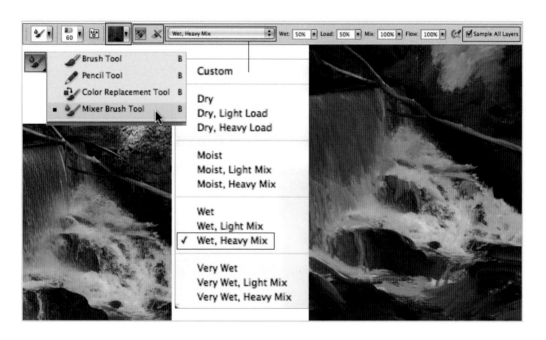

3 Use the Brush Preset Picker or the Brush panel to select and define your brush.

4 Tick Sample All Layers.

5 Choose a mixture preset from the menu or set parameters for Wet, Load and Mix.

6 Optional: enable Airbrush and set Flow, and toggle options to load or clean the brush after each stroke as desired.

7 Option/Alt-click in the image to load the brush.

8 Use the Brush Load menu (next to the Brush panel icon) to load solid colours only and to clean the brush.

 HOT TIP: You can sample and mix colours on a blank part of the document or in a separate window the way you would on a painter's palette, then sample those colours to paint in the image.

Use bristle tips

Bristle tips are new to Photoshop CS5. They simulate a variety of physical brushes and work best with a graphics tablet because they emulate how brushes respond to physical manipulation. An optional preview window shows what the brush looks like in action and the cursor takes on the shape of the bristles. While a simple round, soft-edged brush might be sufficient for most masking and retouching work, bristle tips allow you to make more interpretive and painterly work.

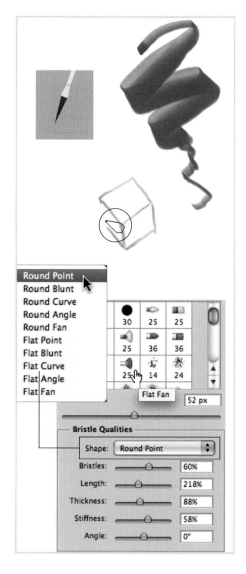

1 Activate the Brush tool.

2 Click the Brush panel icon in the Options bar.

3 Select any bristle tip brush from the list in the panel.

4 Adjust bristle qualities.

5 Select or sample a foreground colour and paint in the image editing area.

? DID YOU KNOW?

Every stroke in the illustration shown here was made with a single brush setup, including brush size. The red figure was made in a single zigzag gesture from top to bottom, using pressure and tilt. The colour change was a simple foreground/background swap.

Shift-drag and Shift-click to keep lines straight

It is difficult to keep lines straight when painting freehand. To paint perfect horizontal or vertical lines, hold the mouse button down, then hold the Shift key down and drag in either a horizontal or a vertical direction.

You can use the following technique to paint straight lines at any angle. The technique works for any brush-based tool, including the Eraser.

1 Pick a starting point, and click the mouse button to make your first mark.

2 Position the cursor somewhere else in the image.

3 While holding the Shift key down, click the mouse button again to draw a connecting line.

4 Shift-click in a third location to draw a connecting line from the previous end-point.

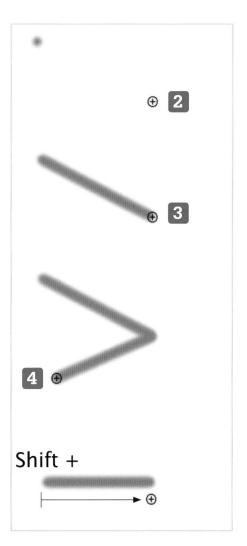

Shift +

 HOT TIP: When using Shift + drag to paint straight lines, the direction stays locked in until you release the Shift key. The mouse pointer can stray way off the line, and your line will remain true. If you release the Shift key and depress it again before you release the mouse, the line will stray and then snap back to its original course.

 SEE ALSO: You can use guides with Snap turned on to help position your marks when you use Shift-click. See Chapter 6.

Use the Brush panel

Use the Brush panel to customise brushes. Once defined, you can use them on the fly or save them as new brush or tool presets.

The Brush panel becomes available via the Options bar whenever you activate a brush-based tool. Even if your Brush panel is hidden, it will appear when you click on the Brush panel icon. To close the Brush panel, click on the double arrow at the top right corner of its tab set.

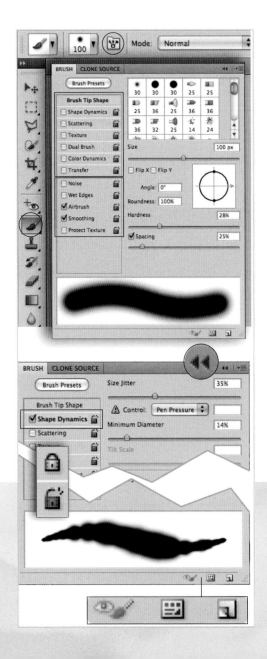

The left side of the panel shows a box containing option sets and parameters. The right side shows the controls for the currently selected option set. Option sets are applied when the box is ticked. Clicking the text in the box (e.g. Scattering) sets the tick mark next to it. Click the box to untick it.

1 Click Brush Tip Shape in the left side of the panel to select a brush tip and alter its size, shape, hardness and spacing.

2 Click Shape Dynamics on the left side of the panel to adjust size jitter, angle jitter and roundness jitter as needed.

3 Use other option sets to affect scattering, texture, dual brush, colour dynamics and transfer.

4 Set parameters that do not have options: noise, wet edges, airbrush mode, path smoothing and protect texture. Clicking the text on these items toggles the tick box.

5 Click the lock icon to retain and apply option sets and parameters (e.g. the current size jitter and airbrush) to the next brush tip that you select.

6 Click the icons at the bottom of the panel to toggle the bristle brush preview, save a new preset or open the Preset Manager.

7 Adjust settings in the Options bar and open the Tool Preset picker to save a new Tool preset.

? DID YOU KNOW?

Shape Dynamics, Opacity, Flow and other features can be controlled through a graphics tablet.

Use Tool presets

Where Brush presets only record the shape of the brush, Tool presets record the tool definition and the Options bar settings. They can also record the current foreground colour, which makes it easy to switch to the 10-pixel red pencil, for example.

1 Click on the icon in the Options bar to open the Tool Preset picker.

2 Click a preset to apply those settings to the tool.

3 Untick Current Tool Only to see all Tool presets.

4 Click the New Tool Preset icon to add a preset.

5 Use the menu to open the Preset Manager and perform management tasks.

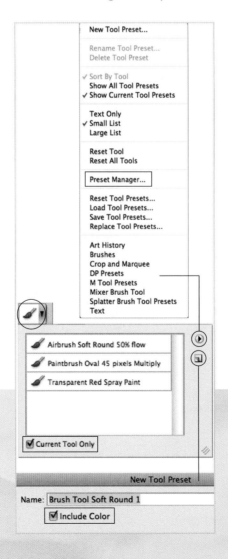

Use the Preset Manager

Brushes and Tools are only two of the eight types of preset that you can save in Photoshop. Use the Preset Manager to load and save brush sets, reorganise the preset list, or delete presets from the list.

1 Select Edit, Preset Manager to open the dialogue.

2 Select the type of preset you wish to work with from the Type menu.

3 Click the triangle and use the menu to change the way the list is displayed and append, reset or replace the library shown in the Preset Manager dialogue and pickers.

4 Drag items in the list to reorganise it.

5 Select one or more items in the list and click Save Set ... to create a new library (e.g. create a library containing only custom bristle tips).

6 Click Load ... to select a library and append it to the bottom of the list.

7 Select one or more items in the list and click Rename ... to revise the name.

8 Select one or more items from the list and click Delete to remove them from the list.

9 Click Done to exit the dialogue.

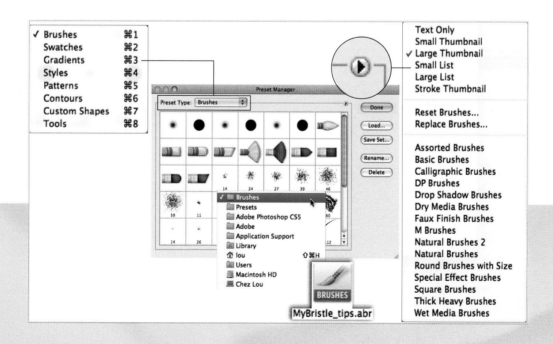

8 Work with selections

Introduction

Selections are an essential tool for harnessing Photoshop's power. Just as you select a layer before performing an operation upon it, you can select regions of the image to modify or duplicate. Selections can be used to constrain painting, filling and deleting, and they can also be used as the basis for creating masks.

Selections can be simple geometric shapes, or based upon the tones or colours in your image. Pixels can be partially selected to produce soft-edged effects. Selections can also be combined and modified in many ways, and they can be translated into masks and alpha channels, which can in turn be translated back into selections.

In the same way that you use a screwdriver and a saw for different tasks, Photoshop offers a range of tools for making different types of selection. Some will finish the job at hand a lot faster than others.

Use the Marquee tools

The Marquee tools are the most rudimentary of the selection tools, but you are likely to use them again and again.

1. To activate the Marquee tool: tap M, use Shift + M to rotate through the tools, or select a Marquee tool from the fly-out menu.

2. Drag diagonally in any direction to create the selection.

3. Hold the Shift key down to make perfect squares or circles.

4. Hold the Option/Alt key to drag from the centre of something.

5. 'Marching ants' appear when you release the mouse button to show the selection.

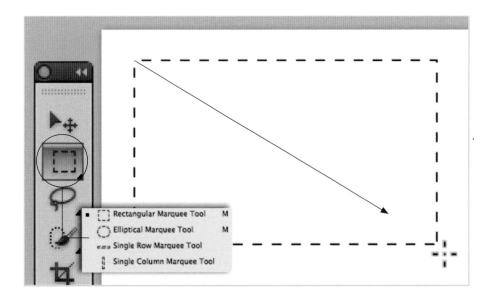

 HOT TIP: The cursor for the Marquee tool is very small. If you lose sight of it, hold down the space bar to show the Hand tool cursor. Wiggle the mouse if you need to. Once you find your mouse pointer, position it where you need it and then release the space bar.

Reposition a selection

You can move any selection by activating the Marquee tool and dragging. When you position the Marquee tool's mouse pointer over an active selection, its icon will change to show that the selection can be dragged. All selections behave in the same manner once they're created; it doesn't matter what tool was used.

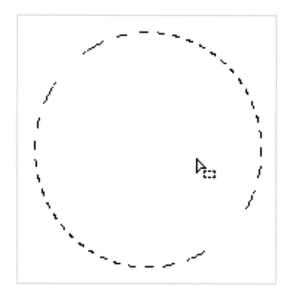

! ALERT: The Move tool will drag pixels, not the selection.

Modify Quick Mask preferences

The Quick Mask mode allows you to visualise selections as a coloured overlay, instead of marching ants. It's being covered early in this chapter, because we'll use it to illustrate a number of techniques along the way. Later in this chapter, we'll cover some other applications of Quick Mask.

The default Quick Mask settings display a translucent red overlay that isn't always easy to read. We'll change the setting to make the Quick Mask show the selected areas as a bright green silhouette.

1. In the Tools panel, double-click on the Quick Mask icon to open the Quick Mask Options dialogue.

2. Click Selected Areas so that the dot appears in the circle next to it.

3. In the Color section, change the opacity to 100 per cent and click on the colour chip to display the colour picker dialogue.

4. Select a colour such as fluorescent green (e.g. #66ff00), which is likely to stand out clearly against almost any image that you can possibly edit. Click OK to accept your colour choice.

5. Click OK to accept the Quick Mask Options.

6. Note that the Quick Mask icon is darkened, the document title contains the words 'Quick Mask', and the active layer is highlighted in grey. These indicate that you are still in Quick Mask mode.

7. Tap the Q key to exit Quick Mask mode.

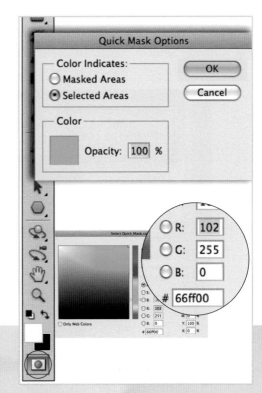

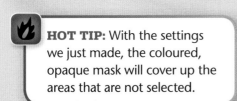

HOT TIP: With the settings we just made, the coloured, opaque mask will cover up the areas that are not selected.

Modify a selection

Selecting parts of an image often involves making an approximate selection and then refining it by degrees. Photoshop has some simple and direct tools to do that.

Use feathering to soften edges when cutting elements out of a layer, so that they blend better with the items they are placed on top of. You can feather your selection with a preview in the Refine Edge dialogue.

The example here shows a selection in Quick Mask mode before and after applying a 30-pixel feather. This is a much higher value than would normally be used; it's just for illustration purposes.

Several techniques for modifying selections include the following:

1 Ctrl-click/right-click in the selection to reveal a menu with options that include Select Inverse, Feather ... and Refine Edge ...

2 In the menu bar, go to Select, Modify, and chose one of the items in the sub-menu, such as Expand.

3 Choose Select, Transform Selection from the menu bar to reshape the selection.

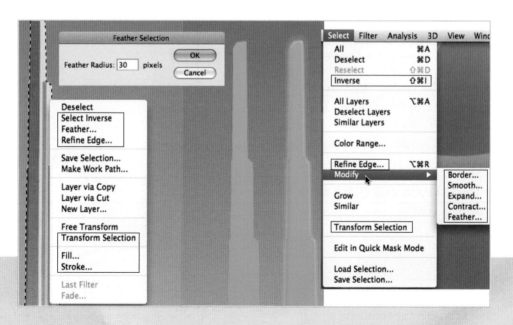

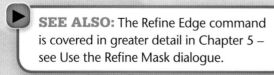

SEE ALSO: The Refine Edge command is covered in greater detail in Chapter 5 – see Use the Refine Mask dialogue.

Use Select, Inverse

Sometimes it's a lot easier to select what you don't want, and then invert the selection. The menu command Select, Inverse (Shift + Command/Ctrl + I) does just that: what was previously unselected becomes selected, and what was previously selected becomes deselected.

1 Notice the 'marching ants' around the edges of the selection before and after using Select, Inverse. You can generally see a difference – look at the edges of your image – but the differences can be subtle.

2 Optional: tap Q to view your selection in Quick Mask mode, then tap Q again to exit Quick Mask. You can do this before and after you invert the selection.

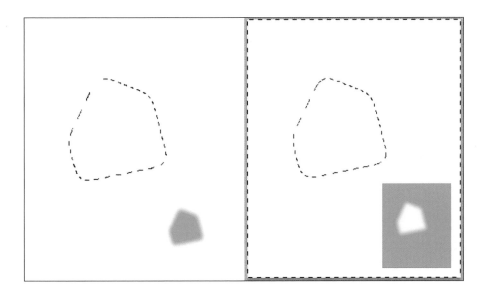

> ⚠️ **ALERT:** There is a very different, but similar-sounding command that inverts pixels: Image, Adjustments, Invert (Command/Ctrl + I). If you accidentally choose that command, just use Command/Ctrl + Z to undo.

Fill, stroke or paint inside selection

To constrain where paint is applied or protect certain areas of your image, it can be helpful to make a selection beforehand – only the selected pixels will be altered. When the selection is feathered, the 'marching ants' appear at the point where the pixels are 50 per cent selected. When the selection is complex, the moving pattern of the selection can be distracting, so there is a way to hide it. The selection in this example was made by loading one of the channels in the image. This technique will be covered at the end of the chapter.

1 Use Command/Ctrl + H (menu: View, Extras) to hide or show Extras, including the 'marching ants'.

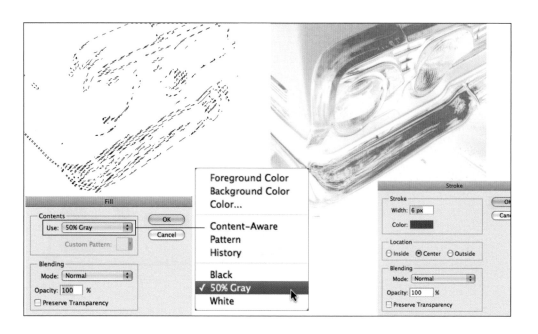

2 Paint on the layer as you normally would. Paint only 'sticks' to the areas that are selected. Partially selected areas will receive translucent colour.

3 Use Option/Alt + Delete/Backspace to fill the selection with the foreground colour from the Tools panel.

4 Use command/Ctrl + Delete/Backspace to fill the selection with the background colour.

5 Select Edit, Fill ... from the menu bar to use the Fill dialogue.

6 In the Fill dialogue, choose one of the preset colours or select Color ... from the Use menu to open the colour picker.

7 Select Edit, Stroke ... from the menu bar to outline the selection. Click the colour box to open the colour picker.

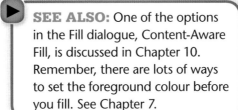

SEE ALSO: One of the options in the Fill dialogue, Content-Aware Fill, is discussed in Chapter 10. Remember, there are lots of ways to set the foreground colour before you fill. See Chapter 7.

Use Lasso tools

The Lasso is a free-form selection tool that is best for loose, irregular selections. In this section, we will discuss the free-form and Polygonal Lassos.

1 Tap L or use Shift + L or use the menu in the Tools panel to select either the Lasso tool or the Polygonal Lasso.

2 Feathering is optional, since you can feather the selection afterwards.

3 Drag out a shape with the Lasso, or click at angle points to create shapes with the Polygonal Lasso.

4 Optional: hold the Option/Alt key down to convert the Lasso into the Polygonal Lasso or vice versa on the fly. Release the key to revert.

5 When you bring the cursor back to the starting point, the cursor will change to indicate that it is ready to close the shape.

6 Click the mouse button to close the shape. Marching ants will appear.

7 If your shape starts to get out of hand, hit the escape key to cancel what you have done so far or deselect with Command/Ctrl + D, and start again.

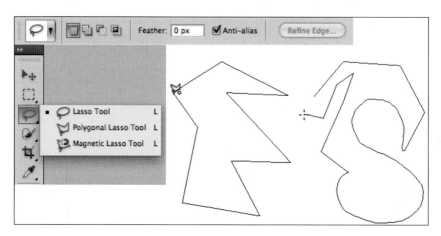

! ALERT: It's generally best to use Anti-Aliasing with any of the selection tools that have it as an option, including the Lasso tools and the Elliptical Marquee. You cannot add anti-aliasing after you have created the selection.

? DID YOU KNOW?
You can use the Pen tool to define and save paths that can easily be converted into selections. Paths can be used to define very precise curves and can be modified more easily and extensively than saved selections.

Use the Quick Selection tool

While many people refer to the Magic Wand tool as the 'Tragic Wand', its sibling – the Quick Selection tool – lives up to its name and largely does what people expected the Magic Wand to do: it intelligently selects parts of the image quickly as you paint a selection. The Quick Selection tool does a much better job at finding edges and completely selecting areas without leaving the little holes that the Magic Wand is known for. When the tool grabs an area that you don't want, you can switch to subtract mode and clear that part of the selection.

While the Quick Selection tool can do a good job on its own, you can think of it as a tool for making a rough selection that you will refine with other tools (e.g. Refine Edge) afterwards.

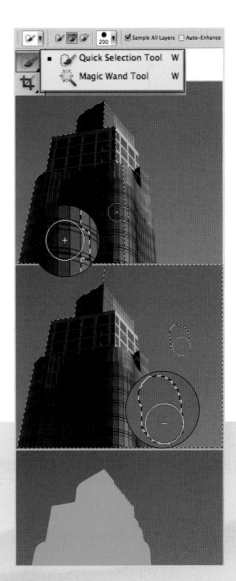

1. To activate, select it from the menu in the Tools panel or tap W or Shift + W to cycle from the Magic Wand.

2. Optional: tick Sample All Layers in the Options bar to make a selection based on all layers in the image, instead of the currently selected layer.

3. Optional: tick Auto-Enhance to reduce roughness and blockiness in the selection boundary.

4. Adjust the brush size: tap the [and] (square bracket) keys, or hold down Ctrl + Option (Windows: Alt + right-click) and drag left or right.

5. Paint over the areas that you want to select. If you release the mouse button and start painting again, the tool will select additional areas.

6. Hold the Option/Alt key down and paint to remove areas.

7. Optional: tap Q to toggle the Quick Mask and check your edges.

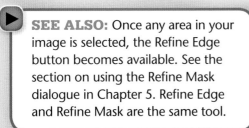

SEE ALSO: Once any area in your image is selected, the Refine Edge button becomes available. See the section on using the Refine Mask dialogue in Chapter 5. Refine Edge and Refine Mask are the same tool.

Add to or subtract from a selection

You can make complex selections by building them up from smaller, simpler selections, starting from a rough selection and refining it step by step. If you're trying to mask someone out of a background, for example, you can start with one set of tools to select the hair precisely, then use a different set of tools to select the body and build upon the hair selection. In other cases, you might start with a loose selection and then whittle away areas that you don't want.

Each of the selection tools has buttons in the Options bar to add or subtract from the current selection. The default setting for most tools is to create a new selection, but the Quick Selection tool adds to the selection by default. All of the selection modes have keyboard shortcuts, indicated in parentheses. The cursor changes shape to indicate the selection mode.

Make an initial selection with any tool, and then make additional selections using the following modes as needed:

1 Use Add to selection (Shift) to append the selection.

2 Use Subtract from selection (Option/Alt) to remove areas.

3 Use Intersect with selection (Shift + Option/Alt) to select the region that both selections have in common.

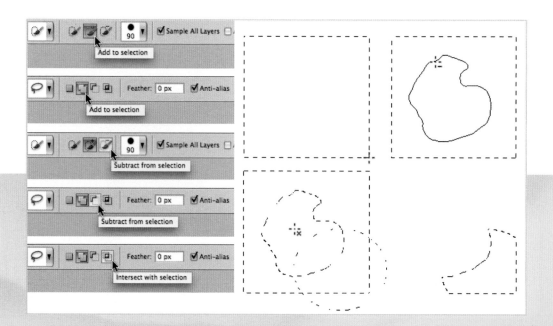

Modify a selection with Quick Mask

You can use Quick Mask to add to, subtract from, or feather a selection. This example shows only a few techniques that can be applied to quick masks and assumes you have set your Quick Mask preferences as shown earlier in this chapter. With those settings, painting in black adds to the selection and painting in white subtracts from it. Start with any selection and tap the Q key to enter Quick Mask.

1 Select Filter, Blur, Gaussian Blur ... from the menu bar to feather the edges.

2 Activate the Brush tool, and choose a moderate size and 50 per cent hardness.

3 Tap the D key to set default colours. (In Quick Mask, the colours are black foreground, white background.)

4 Set the blending mode of the brush to Color Burn and paint in black along the edge of part of the image to harden it.

5 Set the blending mode of the brush back to Normal and increase the hardness to 100 per cent.

6 Tap the X key to swap foreground and background colours.

7 Paint in white inside the coloured area to punch out hard-edged shapes.

8 Create a selection with the Polygonal Lasso tool and fill it with black.

9 Tap the Q key to exit Quick Mask mode. Your selection will appear as marching ants.

HOT TIP: When you enter Quick Mask mode, Photoshop displays the selection as editable pixels. You can perform virtually any operation upon those pixels that you would with any pixel layer, including painting, erasing, warping, moving and applying filters.

Create a new selection with Quick Mask

The Quick Mask tool can easily be used to paint a selection by eye. There is a slight twist to seeing how your mask is fitting: temporarily invert the mask and look for gaps. You can also change your Quick Mask preferences to show a translucent overlay.

1 Tap the Q key to enter Quick Mask mode.

2 Tap the D key to set default colours: black foreground, white background.

3 Vary the brush size and hardness as needed to paint with black over the part of the image that you want to select. You can also paint at lower opacity and flow to build up coverage. Don't worry if you overshoot.

4 To see if you have over-painted any edges, hit Command/Ctrl + I to invert the mask (menu: Image, Adjustments, Invert).

5 Optional: double-click the Quick Mask icon to edit the Quick Mask preferences and reduce the opacity. You may have to tap Q to go back into Quick Mask once you OK the dialogue.

6 Paint with black to colour in areas, and white to remove colour. (Tap X to swap foreground and background colours.)

7 Invert the mask again with Command/Ctrl + I.

8 When your Quick Mask is complete, tap the Q key to exit, and note the marching ants.

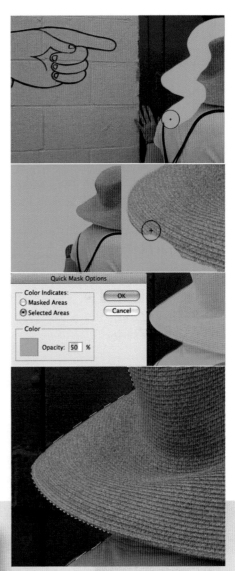

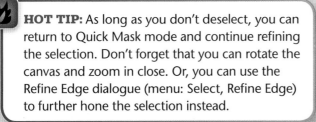

HOT TIP: As long as you don't deselect, you can return to Quick Mask mode and continue refining the selection. Don't forget that you can rotate the canvas and zoom in close. Or, you can use the Refine Edge dialogue (menu: Select, Refine Edge) to further hone the selection instead.

Select by Color Range

Did you ever want to select just the sky in a photo, or everything that wasn't the sky? Or perhaps you want to select someone's face by using skin tones. This is the tool to do just that. Choose Select, Color Range ... from the menu bar to open the dialogue. This example demonstrates a general workflow.

1 Leave Select set to Sampled Colors.

2 Leave the box labelled Localized Color Clusters unticked.

3 Make sure the dot is in the circle labelled Image.

4 Set the Selection Preview to Quick Mask.

5 Start with a Fuzziness of approximately 30.

6 Click in the dialogue box or in the image to select an initial colour.

7 Shift-click to select more colours and use Command/Ctrl + Z to undo a stray sample.

8 Option/Alt-click to subtract colours.

9 Refine your selection by adjusting the Fuzziness slider.

10 Click OK.

ALERT: It's generally best to keep the fuzziness low and take more colour samples. Setting the Fuzziness too high can select areas you don't want and decreasing it too much can result in a jagged selection.

Save a selection

Once you've spent more than a minute or two creating a complex selection, you can appreciate how useful it might be to be able to save and reuse them. When you save a selection, it is stored as an Alpha Channel, which appears in the Channels panel. If you select a layer that has a mask (e.g. a Curves adjustment layer) before you save the selection, you have options for using the selection to create a new layer mask.

To open the dialogue, choose Select, Save Selection ... from the menu bar. Below are some ways of working with saved selections:

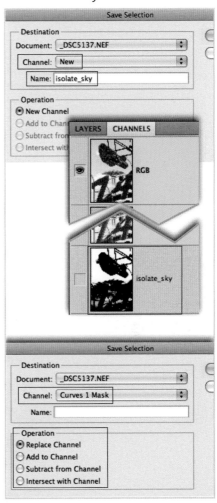

1 With the Channel menu set to New, enter a name and click OK to save your selection.

2 Select the active layer's mask from the Channel menu and select an operation. Click OK to revise the mask.

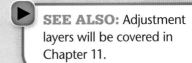

▶ SEE ALSO: Adjustment layers will be covered in Chapter 11.

Load a selection

Saved selections are stored as Alpha Channels within your file, and can be loaded and reused at any time. An example from earlier in this chapter showed how you could use a selection created by loading one of the colour channels. Those colour channels are another kind of Alpha Channel, and layer masks are a third type of Alpha Channel. You can load any Alpha Channel as a selection. If a layer has transparent elements, you can also make a selection based on the opacity of the layer's pixels.

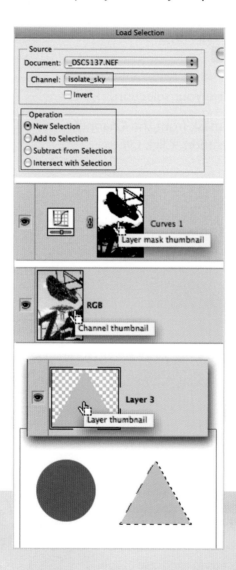

1 To load a saved selection, choose Select, Load Selection … from the menu bar:

- The Load Selection dialogue will appear.
- Select a channel from the menu (only saved selections will appear).
- Choose an operation.
- Optional: tick the box marked Invert to load the inverse selection.
- Click OK.

2 To load a layer mask as a selection, Command/Ctrl-click on its thumbnail. The mouse pointer changes shape to indicate that the selection will be loaded.

3 Open the Channels panel and Command/Ctrl-click on any thumbnail to load it as a selection.

- Loading a saved selection through the Channels panel is the same as using the Load Selection dialogue.
- Loading the RGB channel creates a selection based on tonality. This is a very useful selection to make as a precursor to adding Curves.

4 To load a layer's opacity as a selection, Command/Ctrl-click on its thumbnail.

 HOT TIP: After all this discussion, the selection tool that wasn't mentioned isn't really a tool at all, it's a command: Select, All (Command/Ctrl + A). It forms a sort of bookend with Select, Deselect (Command/Ctrl + D), and you may be surprised how frequently you use both commands.

9 Crop, erase, undo

Introduction

In Chapter 3, we looked at how you can crop in Camera Raw at the beginning of the workflow. That's a good place to do it, but Camera Raw can't edit Photoshop files or layered TIFFs, and there will be times when it makes more sense to crop later in the process anyway. In CS5, Photoshop's crop tool has some new options that distinguish it further from its Camera Raw sibling.

Despite all the emphasis on non-destructive editing and using masks to hide rather than remove pixels, there are still good reasons to erase. There are also times when editing goes awry, and you discover that you've erased or deleted something that you still need. The History panel can provide a wide array of methods, beyond a simple undo, for rolling your work back.

Crop or trim an image

The Trim command will snip blank edges from your image based on transparency or colour. Select Image, Trim from the menu bar to use it. You can use the Crop tool to simply trim edges from your canvas, or to reshape it completely. A lot of photographers crop as a way of removing unwanted items from an image, but that can leave an unbalanced composition. Photoshop CS5 introduces a 'Rule of Thirds' grid (an OpenGL feature) to help you crop with composition in mind.

1 Tap C or click in the Tool panel to activate the Crop tool.

2 If the Width, Height or Resolution fields contain values, press the Clear button.

3 Drag diagonally to select an approximate area to crop and release the mouse button. The Options bar will update.

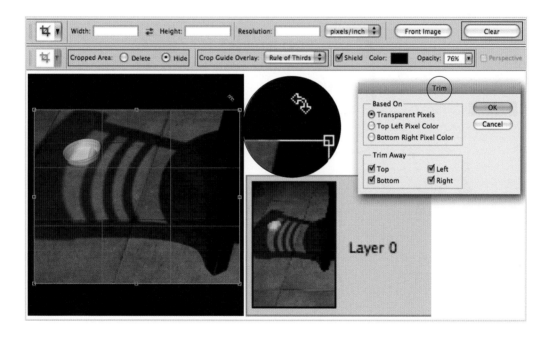

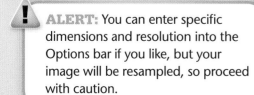

ALERT: You can enter specific dimensions and resolution into the Options bar if you like, but your image will be resampled, so proceed with caution.

4 To retain the cropped pixels in your image, set the Cropped Area to Hide; otherwise, set it to Delete. (If your image only contains a Background layer, hold down Option/Alt and double-click the background to convert it to use Hide.)

5 Optional: choose a Crop Guide Overlay to aid in composition or None.

6 Optional: toggle the shield on or off and adjust opacity and colour as needed. The shield covers up the part of the image that will be hidden or discarded.

7 Drag the handles to reshape the crop. Hold the Shift key and drag the corner handles to scale the crop and retain the same shape. Use the arrow keys to nudge the crop location. Move the mouse pointer outside the corners and drag to crop and rotate the image.

8 Hit the Return/Enter key to apply the cropping.

9 Optional: if you cropped with the Hide option, use the Move tool to reposition the crop and reveal hidden areas or select Image, Reveal All to remove the crop.

? DID YOU KNOW?

Another way of cropping an image is to make a selection with one of the Marquee tools and choose Image, Crop from the menu.

Erase

The Eraser tool is straightforward, but has subtle variations to be aware of. For example, you can use the edge of a soft eraser to create a feathered effect. Most significantly, the Eraser is a brush – you can use any tip with it to create artistic effects such as erosion. Remember that erasing permanently deletes pixels, where painting parts of a mask black produces the same effect. When a mask is no longer useful, you can even erase with it. You can also make large, loose selections and clear them with a keystroke.

1 Select the Eraser tool (tap E) and set its Mode, Opacity and Flow via the Options bar.

2 Use the Eraser in Brush mode and paint with brush tips for effects such as feathered edges or erosion. Use reduced Opacity and Flow as needed.

3 Zoom in and use the Eraser in Block mode to clear areas pixel by pixel.

4 Make a selection (e.g. with the Lasso or Marquee tools) and hit the Delete/Backspace key to clear pixels or use the selection to confine where you erase. Don't forget to deselect (Command/Ctrl + D) afterwards.

5 Ctrl-click/right-click on a layer mask and select Apply Layer Mask from the menu to erase the masked pixels and discard the mask.

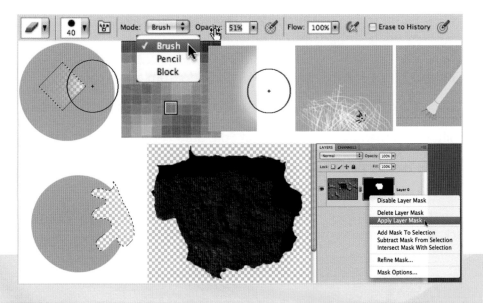

SEE ALSO: Chapter 8 covers selections and Chapter 5 covers layers and masks. You can use the Eraser with the History panel. See the next section for more information.

HOT TIP: You can use a graphics tablet to control the Eraser's opacity and size with pen pressure.

Use undo, redo and the History panel

From the point that you open a file until you close it, Photoshop maintains a transcript of your edits. Each change to your file is recorded as a new state in the History panel. When you undo a change with Command/Ctrl + Z, Photoshop reverts to the previous state, but if you undo again immediately, Photoshop performs a redo and restores the state you started from. If you want to step back to earlier states, you can use a different keystroke or click in the History panel.

Because history states consume memory and affect performance, Photoshop only remembers 20 states by default before it starts recycling – it discards the oldest state to make room for the next new state. You can change a preference so that Photoshop records more history states, and you can also record snapshots, which won't automatically be discarded. However, all history states and snapshots are discarded whenever you close a file.

When you select an earlier history state, the file reverts to that state and the subsequent states in the panel are dimmed. You can selectively undo or redo parts of the image by painting with the History brush or by setting the Use menu to History when you select Edit, Fill from the menu bar. If you discover that you've lost a layer and it's only in your snapshot states, you can recover it: create a new document from that state, split the screens, and drag the layer back into your work file.

1 Use Command/Ctrl + Z to select Edit, Undo/Redo from the menu bar.

2 Use Option/Alt + Command/Ctrl + Z to select Edit, Step Backward from the menu bar.

3 Use Shift + Command/Ctrl + Z to select Edit, Step Forward from the menu bar.

4 Click on the History panel tab or select Window, History from the menu bar to show the panel.

5 Click on the camera icon at the bottom of the panel to save a snapshot or Option/Alt-click on the icon to name the snapshot when you save it.

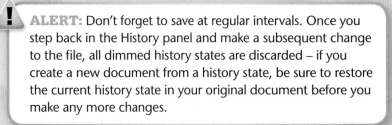

ALERT: Don't forget to save at regular intervals. Once you step back in the History panel and make a subsequent change to the file, all dimmed history states are discarded – if you create a new document from a history state, be sure to restore the current history state in your original document before you make any more changes.

6 Click on the label of a history state or snapshot to revert to that state. To step backwards, click one history state at a time from bottom to top.

7 Click the box on the left edge of the panel to determine where the History Brush and the History option in the Edit, Fill dialogue draw their data from.

8 Activate a history state and click the icon at the bottom of the panel to create a new document from that state. See the alert on p. 200 for more details.

9 Select Photoshop, Preferences, Performance (Windows: Edit, Preferences, Performance) to change the number of history states that Photoshop retains.

10 Choose History Options ... from the panel menu in the upper right corner to set the option to create a new snapshot automatically each time you save.

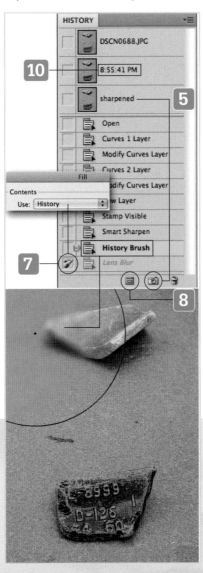

10 Combine, retouch, manipulate

Introduction

You can use the techniques in this chapter along with layer techniques in Chapter 5 and colour and tone techniques in Chapter 11 to create sophisticated combined images. We'll look at several ways of combining and editing image content in this chapter, including some of the fundamental tools and techniques for retouching. Even if you're simply retouching a portrait, the most effective approach is to use layers that can be revised or replaced later.

Part of Photoshop's reputation is based on how artists can use it to composite and 'fake' imagery in a very believable way. A common lament in some circles is that Photoshop makes such things 'too easy'. New CS5 features like Content-Aware Fill and Puppet Warp are likely to fan those flames. The truth is, it still takes vision and skill to make those illusions work, and even more skill to make them seem like they're not illusions. However, the first step towards creating that kind of work is knowing that the tools exist and how to use them.

Load files into Photoshop layers

You can make a selection of thumbnails in either Mini Bridge or Bridge, and then open those files together into a single Photoshop file with one command. The files will load as layers stacked directly above each other, with the layers named after the files they came from. Documents created in this manner do not have a locked Background layer.

To create the example shown here, the two layers were loaded into Photoshop and the layers were reordered so that the layer containing the boy was on top. The opacity of the top layer was reduced temporarily and the layers were moved around until the arrangement looked good. The sand in the layer with the boy was selected via the Color Range command (see Chapter 8), and a mask was made from the selection (see Chapter 5). To make the composition stronger, the Ferris wheel layer was rotated and scaled slightly using the Free Transform command discussed later in this chapter. Curves adjustments (see Chapter 11) were added to brighten and increase contrast where needed, and the mask of one of the curves was painted out over the darker areas to maintain a sense of depth.

To load a selection of files as layers:

1️⃣ In Mini Bridge: select Photoshop, Load Files into Photoshop Layers ... from the Tools menu icon.

2️⃣ In Bridge: select Tools, Photoshop, Load Files into Photoshop Layers ... from the menu bar.

❓ DID YOU KNOW?

If you shoot several bracketed shots of a scene, you can use the Merge to HDR Pro command to combine elements from those exposures into a new image. HDR (high dynamic range) images can have a range of looks from low contrast to surrealistic, and require special shooting techniques for best results. You can apply the new HDR Toning adjustment to a single image to simulate the look of HDR. This feature is discussed on p. 15.

Generate collages and panoramas

Photoshop can do a lot of the work of melding images into panoramas and collages for you. The Photomerge command can automatically match and mask a selected group of images into a cohesive arrangement. From there, you have the option to straighten and enhance the image even further.

1 Select two or more images in either Mini Bridge or Bridge.

2 Select Photoshop, Photomerge … from the Tools menu icon in Mini Bridge or Tools, Photoshop, Photomerge … from the menu bar in Bridge.

3 Use the dialogue box to add or remove files from the list and set processing parameters.

4 Click OK.

5 The resulting file will name the layers based upon the files they came from.

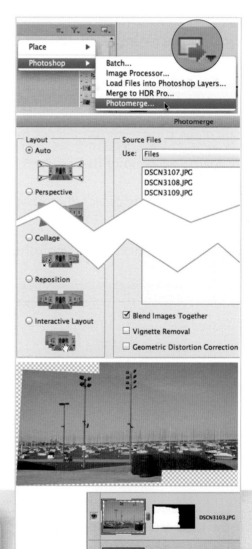

HOT TIP: For best results with panorama stitching, Photoshop needs about 40 per cent overlap. If they overlap 70 per cent or more, they may not blend. It's also best not to move or zoom in or out as you take the frames. Try to keep your panning level and your exposure consistent.

Straighten an image

In older versions of Photoshop, you could use the Ruler tool and then the Image Rotation command to straighten images. The new Straighten button in the Options bar simplifies the process and makes the operation very similar to straightening in Camera Raw. If your image only contains a background layer, you may want to convert it to a normal layer first. Otherwise Photoshop will fill in the edges of your canvas with the current background colour. The illustration here uses the image from the previous example, which already has normal layers.

1 Optional: Option/Alt-double-click on the background to convert it to a conventional layer.

2 Select the Ruler tool: use the button menu in the Tools panel or tap Shift + I repeatedly until the tool appears in the button.

3 Drag in the image to define a horizon line or an element that should be perfectly vertical.

4 Click the Straighten button in the Options bar: Photoshop straightens the image and automatically crops it.

5 To remove the cropping, use Command/Ctrl + Z or choose Edit, Undo from the menu immediately after you straighten.

6 In some cases, rotating the image may push some parts of the image off the visible part of the canvas. Select Image, Reveal All to fix it.

7 The straightened image can also come out rotated 90 degrees from the orientation you want. Select Image, Image Rotation, 90° CW or 90° CCW from the menu bar to rotate clockwise or anti-clockwise as needed.

HOT TIP: The cursor for the Ruler tool is one of several very small cursors. If you lose sight of it, hold down the space bar to turn it into the Hand tool. Position the cursor where you need it, and release the space bar.

Use Content-Aware Fill

Arthur C. Clarke once said that any sufficiently advanced technology is indistinguishable from magic. By that measure, Photoshop's new Content-Aware Fill feature is advanced, and it is easy to use, too. It works by copying and colour-matching data from other parts of the image to fill in the selected area. The results will probably not be perfect, but they will generally get you a lot closer to what you want, quickly and easily.

This example uses Content-Aware Fill to patch the gaps around the edges of the image that were left after the image was straightened in the previous example. Since Content-Aware Fill works on a pixel layer, a composite of the existing layers was stamped, rather than flattening the file. See Chapter 5 for details. After running Content-Aware Fill the first time, part of the dustbin got duplicated in front of the shrub. To repair it, a small selection was made and Content-Aware Fill was run a second time.

1 Command/Ctrl-click on the thumbnail of the layer you want to fill. This loads a selection based on opacity.

2 Choose Select, Inverse from the menu bar. The transparent pixels are now selected.

3 Select Edit, Fill from the menu bar.

4 Set the Use menu to Content-Aware and click OK.

5 Use Command/Ctrl + D to deselect.

6 Use additional retouching tools to finish cleaning up the image.

HOT TIP: Content-Aware Fill often works better when the selection extends into the area you want to replicate. Once you've inverted the selection, you can add to the selection with one of the selection tools (e.g. the Lasso) in Add to Selection mode. Content-Aware Fill randomises content to create its fills. Re-running it on the same area can produce different results each time.

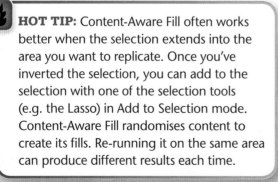

Place files

Drop additional images as new layers, named after the files they came from, into any open document. You can drag multiple files in one shot from Mini Bridge or Bridge, or drag from open windows in other applications, such as the Mac Finder, Windows, your e-mail, etc.

1 Open any image in Photoshop or create a new document.

2 Drag another image on to the editing canvas.

3 The image will be ready to be scaled and positioned: drag into position and use the handles to resize.

4 Hit Return/Enter to commit the placement.

5 Optional: to turn off the Resize or Smart Object options: select Photoshop, Preferences, General (Windows: Edit, Preferences, General) from the menu bar. You can untick the options marked Place or Drag Raster Images as Smart Objects and Resize Image During Place as needed.

 HOT TIP: Photoshop's default behaviour is to place these items into the document as Smart Objects (see Chapter 5). The advantage of Smart Objects is that you can transform them and apply filters non-destructively, but some types of editing are a bit more complicated with Smart Objects, and there may be times when the Smart Objects affect performance. You can rasterise them into normal layers at any time, and you can turn off the option to place files as Smart Objects.

Change the canvas size

One common task is to gang several images to create a diptych or triptych. An easy way to do this is to start with a 'seed' image and then place other images into it, expanding the canvas as needed. You can expand the canvas in absolute or relative proportions, increasing the height, width or both, using a number of measurement scales. In this example, two images will be grouped together with a dividing line between them. The canvas will be expanded in two steps.

1 Open an image that will serve as the seed for the diptych.

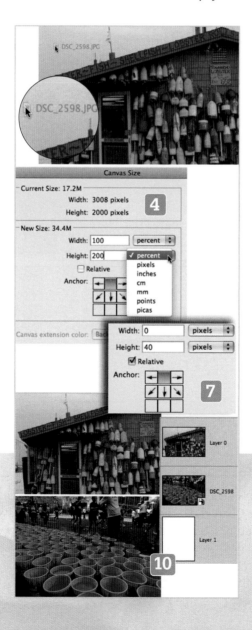

2 Option/Alt-double-click on the background in the Layers panel to convert it to a conventional layer (Layer 0).

3 Drag a second image on to the canvas area to place it into the seed document.

4 Select Image, Canvas Size … from the menu bar.

5 Enter the desired dimensions and direction (e.g. 200 per cent height growing downward from the top centre), and click OK.

6 Tap M to activate the Move tool and position one of the layers at the bottom of the canvas, covering the transparent area to complete the basic diptych with no separation between the images.

To add space between the images do the following:

7 Select Image, Canvas Size … from the menu bar.

8 Tick the box marked Relative and enter a direction and spacing (e.g. 40 pixels from the top centre downwards).

9 Drag the bottom image downwards so that the gap appears between the images.

10 Add a blank layer, drag it to the bottom of the layer stack, and use Edit, Fill to fill it with a colour.

HOT TIP: If you don't convert the background to a normal layer, the expanded part of the canvas will be filled with a solid colour rather than transparent pixels. If you decrease the canvas size and part of your image no longer fits the new canvas size, Photoshop will ask if you want to discard that part of the image. If you would rather hide the pixels, use the Crop tool instead.

Use Free Transform

Free Transform is just one of several transformation modes. You can think of it as a gateway command to all of the transformation modes, because once you invoke Free Transform, you can switch easily to any other mode, including Perspective and Warp. You can transform layers or pixels within a selection.

1 Use Command/Ctrl + T (menu: Edit, Free Transform) to enter Free Transform.

2 Shift-drag corners of the transform frame to scale proportionately; drag corners to stretch and scale.

3 Drag outside the frame to rotate; reposition the reference point to rotate around a specific axis.

4 Hold down the Command/Ctrl key and drag the corner handles to free distort.

5 Option/Alt – drag the handles to expand or contract around the centre.

6 Ctrl-click/right-click in the image and use the menu to select Perspective mode; note the other modes. Drag the corner handles to shift perspective and drag the centre handles to skew.

7 Hit Return/Enter to commit the transformation, or hit Esc to exit.

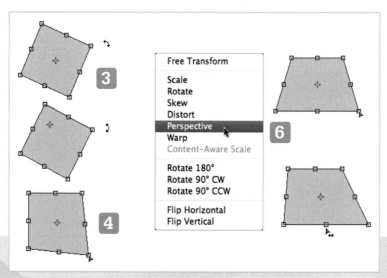

! ALERT: Free Transform can substantially degrade your image. It's a good idea to convert a layer to a Smart Object before transforming it. Otherwise, if you want to perform multiple transformations (e.g. Scale and Warp), switch modes and do both transformations before committing.

Use Free Transform via the Options bar

Aside from manipulating handles in the image, you can enter numeric values into the Options bar to transform elements precisely.

1 Command/Ctrl + T (menu: Edit, Free Transform) to enter Free Transform.

2 Enter X and Y values into the Options bar to adjust position numerically.

3 Use the reference point locator to position the reference point for X and Y.

4 Use the relative position button to specify X and Y relative to the current position.

5 Enter W(idth) and H(eight) into the Options bar to scale numerically: use the chain icon to link W and H for proportional scaling. Use abbreviations – px, in, cm, % – to specify units.

6 Enter an angle to rotate numerically.

7 Enter H(orizontal) and V(ertical) skew values to skew numerically.

8 Click the icon in the Options bar to switch to or from Warp mode; use presets or drag handles and parts of the mesh to warp.

9 Hit Return/Enter to commit the transformation, or hit Esc to exit.

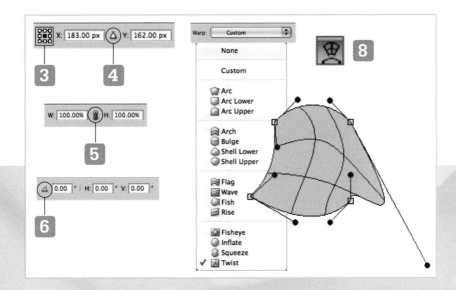

Use the Clone Stamp

The Clone Stamp is a brush-based tool that has the effect of copying and pasting information from one part of your image to another. You point at a location in the image to load the Clone Stamp with source material before you apply it. As you apply the brush, the location of the source tracks along with the brush and information is copied from the source to the brush location. To aid in blending, you can clone at reduced Opacity and Flow, and you can feather the edge of the brush by reducing the Hardness setting. With the Sample All Layers option, you can clone into a blank layer. You can also clone into a layer that contains pixels, using the same blending modes you saw in Chapter 5. The soften wrinkles example in the Top 10 Tips demonstrates some of these techniques.

1 Prepare a layer for cloning: create a new blank layer, stamp a layer, or duplicate a layer that you intend to retouch into (see Chapter 5 for details on layers). Click the layer to select it.

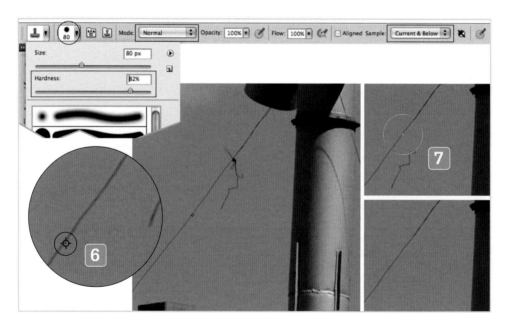

2 Type S or Shift-S to activate the Clone Stamp tool. Be sure you've selected the Clone Stamp, and not the Pattern Stamp, which is under the same button.

3 In the Options panel, set Mode to Normal, and Sample to Current & Below.

4 Set Opacity and Flow as needed.

5 Use the square bracket keys ([and]) to match the size of the brush to the task.

6 Option/Alt-click on a source area to load the Clone Stamp.

7 Use the brush preview to align any elements that need to match as you clone. Press the mouse button down and paint to apply the cloning.

8 Resize the brush and set new sources as you clean up the image.

 HOT TIP: Watch for differences in tone. Cloning from too light a source or too dark a source makes your work very obvious. Often, a moderate hardness level for the Clone Stamp will blend better and make the cloning less conspicuous. If you're using a graphics tablet, check the Brush panel: if Shape Dynamics is turned on, you will have to press firmly to get the brush to grow to the size of the preview.

Use Align

The Clone Stamp and Healing Brush (discussed later in this chapter) both have a tick box marked Aligned in the Options bar. This is a very useful feature that controls where information is copied from, and can make healing or cloning lots of small areas a much easier task.

Whenever you Option/Alt-click in the image, you set a sample point that tells the tool where to start copying from as you apply the brush. After you have set the sample point, and as soon as you hold the mouse button down somewhere in the image, a little crosshair will appear at the sample point, indicating where the brush is copying from. As you drag the mouse across the image, this crosshair will move in a path that parallels the movement of the brush. This behaviour is the same for the first stroke you make, whether Aligned is ticked or not.

Aligned takes effect whenever you make the second and subsequent strokes. If Aligned is turned off, the brush continues to copy from the original starting point. If Aligned is turned on, the brush will move the starting point to a new location each time you start a new stroke, based on where you moved the brush. The preview in the brush tip helps you avoid replicating source areas you don't want, but you can turn it off in the Clone Source panel, if you need to.

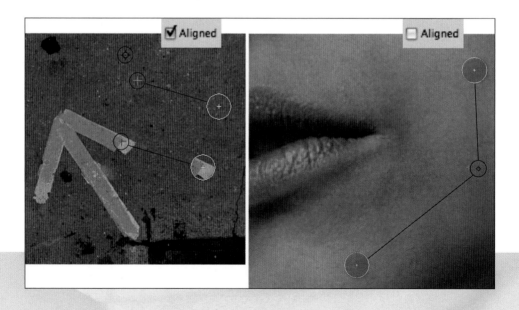

Use the Healing Brush

The Healing Brush tool is a mainstay of retouching. It is essentially a cross between the Patch tool and the Clone Stamp. As with the Clone Stamp, you can paint on to a blank layer or use a blending mode as you paint on to a stamped or duplicate layer (containing pixels).

To use the Healing Brush, you load the brush with a sample first, and then paint over the part that you want to heal. The Healing Brush copies the texture from the area you sampled, and tries to match it to the colour and tone of the area that you're healing.

1 Create a new blank layer for retouching, or reuse an existing retouching layer. Click the layer to select it.

2 Tap J or Shift + J, or use the button menu in the Tools panel to select the Healing Brush.

3 Click the Brush Picker button in the Tool Options panel.

4 Check to see that the hardness slider is at 100 per cent and hit the Return key to put the Brush Picker away.

5 Check the blending mode (default is Normal), and that the circle to the left of Sampled is filled in.

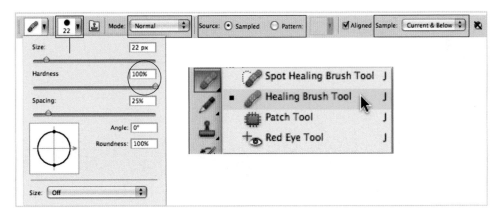

6 Set the Sample menu to read Current & Below.

7 Position the brush over the item that you want to heal, and use the square bracket keys ([and]) to set an appropriate size for the brush. The Healing Brush is now configured.

8 To load the tool with a sample, Option/Alt-click on an area that has the right texture for the area you're healing. Release the Option/Alt key after you release the mouse button.

9 Now, paint the area that you want to heal. Sometimes, you just need to click the brush in one spot, and sometimes you'll need to make short strokes.

HOT TIP: When working with tools like the Healing Brush, you can zoom in to get a closer view of your work, but be careful: if you zoom in too much, you'll find yourself repairing things that won't show up in your print, much less on the web.

? DID YOU KNOW?

The Spot Healing Brush samples automatically, and the new Content-Aware option makes this tool a lot more useful, particularly for tasks like removing power lines or telephone wires from a scene. It's not perfect, and you'll probably need to do some clean-up after you use it, but it's a lot faster than trying to do it all by hand.

Reshape with the Liquify filter

The Liquify filter is very handy for resculpting things, whether it's an arm that's too thin or a bulge that's too thick. With a little imagination, you'll be amazed at the things you can use it for. It's a close relative of the Warp tool, with a distinctive difference: you can save the mesh that defines the transformation you're making and then apply it to other parts of the same image or other images.

Two keys to using the tool are to go slowly, and to pre-select the area that you want to work with, so that Photoshop performs faster. If you save the mesh, be sure to save the selection to apply the identical warp again. This is a destructive edit, so it's best to stamp or duplicate a layer to apply the filter to.

To make a new warp:

1 Hit the M key to activate the Marquee tool and draw a selection around the part of the image that you want to liquify. Try to keep the selection as small as possible, but leave a little extra room around the edges to work.

2 Select Filter, Liquify from the menu. The Liquify dialogue will appear.

3 In the Tool Options section of the dialogue, select a low brush pressure (i.e. 10 or less) and a broad brush. The precise size and pressure of the brush will be determined by the nature of whatever you want to reshape. Use the square bracket keys ([and]) to adjust brush size.

4 Select the Forward Warp tool from the panel at the left side of the dialogue.

5 Optional: tick the Show Backdrop box and adjust the Opacity to see how your warp fits with the image.

6 Using short to medium strokes, slowly push the edges of the part of the body that you want to reshape.

7 Optional: save your mesh file – click Save Mesh … and use the system dialogue to save.

8 Click the OK button to commit your changes.

HOT TIP: The Liquify tool will also warp the area around whatever you're reshaping. If you use this on a person who is standing in front of something with a strong pattern, you might have to extract the person on to their own layer to do the liquify and patch the pattern to make it believable. Content-Aware Fill can be useful for fixing the pattern in some cases.

To reapply a liquify:

9 Reposition or load a saved selection as needed.

10 Load your saved mesh to reapply – click Load Mesh … and use the system dialogue to navigate to a saved mesh file and open it.

11 Revise the liquify as needed.

12 Click OK to commit the changes.

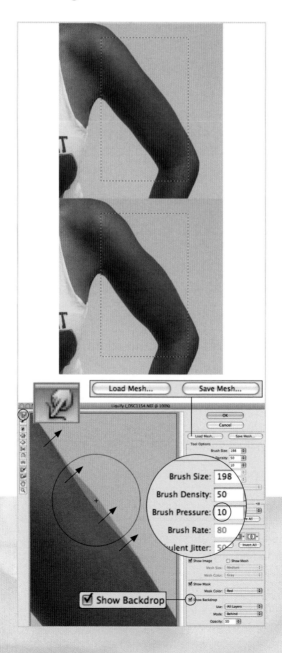

Use Puppet Warp

Puppet Warp is a clever feature that allows you to distort an image by manipulating an elastic structural mesh. You place pins in the mesh to lock down parts of the image, and then drag one or more pins to reshape other parts of the image. You can turn off the mesh display if it's distracting, and use the grid display to aid in alignment. Use the Mode menu to adjust the elasticity of the mesh, and the Density menu to adjust the precision of the transformation.

If you extract a figure from its background, you can use Puppet Warp to distort the figure even more dramatically without telltale distortion in the background. While it has obvious application for subtly straightening elements, it can also be used artistically to distort images intentionally in ways that the Liquify and Warp tools cannot.

1 To activate, select Edit, Puppet Warp from the menu bar.

2 Click in the image to place pins.

3 Click pins to select them (a black dot appears). Shift-click to select additional pins.

4 Hit Delete/Backspace to remove selected pins.

5 Hold down the H key to hide pins temporarily.

6 Optional: select View, Show, Grid from the menu bar (keyboard: Command/Ctrl + ') to toggle the grid. Click Show Mesh in the Options bar to show or hide the mesh.

7 Drag pins to reshape the image.

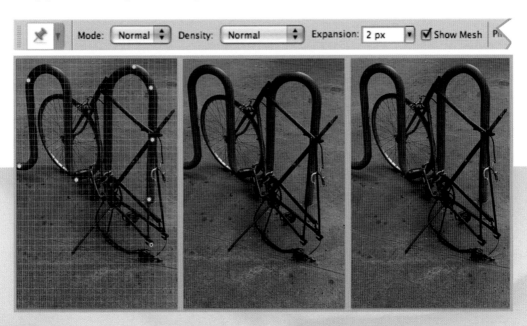

8 To rotate around a pin: select a pin and Option/Alt drag outside the pin. Degrees will appear in the Options bar.

9 Use Command-Z to undo the last move.

10 Hit Return/Enter to commit the transformation.

 HOT TIP: It's best to apply Puppet Warp to a smart object, or use it to transform a duplicate or stamped layer.

11 Adjust colour and tone

Use the Adjustments panel and presets

The Adjustments panel has two modes: in the list view, it serves as a launch pad to add adjustment layers to your image. When an adjustment layer is selected in the Layers panel, it displays the controls for that layer. Click on the Adjustments tab in the Dock or select Window, Adjustments from the menu bar to display the panel.

In the list view:

1 Click an icon button to add an adjustment layer.

2 Click a triangle in the list to expand or collapse a group of presets.

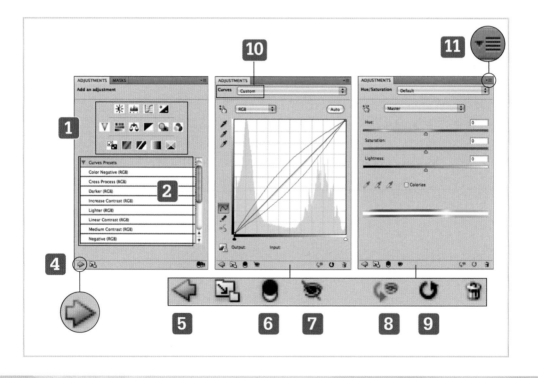

3 Click on an item from the preset list to add that adjustment.

4 Click the right-facing arrow to return to the controls for the current adjustment layer.

In the control view:

5 Click the left-facing arrow to return to the list view.

6 Click the overlapping circle icon to clip the adjustment to the layer beneath it or to unclip it. (See Use a clipping mask later in this chapter.)

7 Click the eyeball icon to show or hide the effect of the adjustment.

8 Hold down the indicated button or hold the \ key to view the previous adjustment setting.

9 Click the revolving arrow icon to go back to the previous setting. Click it a second time to reset the dialogue.

10 Use the menu at the top of the dialogue to use a preset or default settings.

11 Use the panel menu in the upper right corner of the dialogue to manage presets.

Adjust contrast with a preset curve

Preset curve adjustments provide a quick and simple way to improve the appearance of a photo. When you add an adjustment layer, it is added directly above the currently selected layer.

1 In the Layer panel, select a layer to determine where the adjustment layer will be added.

2 Show the Adjustments panel and switch to the list view.

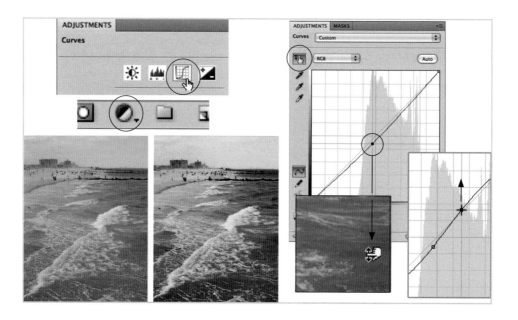

 HOT TIP: Often, as you increase contrast in a colour photo, the saturation increases, and there are times where it can increase too much. You can compensate for that by adding a Hue/Saturation layer. See details later in this chapter.

3 Click the triangle to display the list of Curves presets.

4 Click a preset, such as Strong Contrast (RGB), to apply it. The adjustment layer will appear in the Layers panel, and the Adjustments panel will switch to the curve controls.

Optional:

5 Use the menu at the top of the Adjustments panel to test other presets.

6 Move the control points in the curve to modify the adjustment.

7 Toggle layer visibility with the eyeball icon to compare before and after.

8 Use the panel menu in the upper right corner to save a custom preset.

Make a Curves adjustment layer from scratch

Presets can be helpful, but there are times when modifying the preset can take as much effort as doing the curve from nothing. You can create a curve using the targeted adjustment tool in the Curves controls, or click and drag in the graph.

1 Select a layer to define where the Curves adjustment will be added.

2 Click on the icon to add a Curves adjustment layer in the Adjustments panel or select Curves from the black and white circle menu at the bottom of the Layers panel.

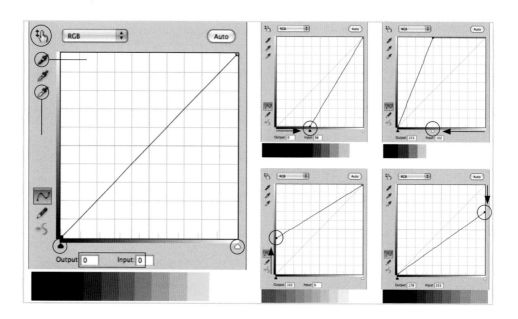

3 To toggle the targeted adjustment feature, click on the finger icon on the left side of the Adjustments panel. The button will darken when it is activated.

4 To use a targeted adjustment, position the cursor over an area in the image where you think the tones should be lighter or darker, and drag up or down in the image. The corresponding point on the curve will move. Release the mouse when you are satisfied with the adjustment. Click the targeted adjustment button to toggle it off.

5 Click the tone line to add a point.

6 Tap + or – (plus or minus keys) to select the next or previous point in the curve.

7 Click a point to select it and Shift-click to select additional points.

8 Drag points up or down, or use arrow keys, to lighten or darken.

9 To delete points, hit the Delete/Backspace key or drag the point until it pops off the line.

10 Option/Alt-click on the grid to switch between quarter-tone and Zone System grids.

 HOT TIP: Curves can do everything that Levels does and more. It makes Levels obsolete. Place a point in the middle of the curve and drag diagonally to create the same effect as the gamma slider in Levels.

Adjust the black point and white point

In situations where the lighting or the exposure have made the blacks in an image weak, moving the black point to the right can add weight and dramatically improve the image. Similarly, dull highlights can be improved by moving the white point to the left. Either of these moves will also increase the contrast in your image. Used less frequently are two moves that reduce contrast: moving the black point up creates a washed-out effect that can be good for creating background images, and moving the white point down greys out the highlights. The original grey ramp is shown on the left and the effect of each adjustment is shown beneath the graph. After adjusting the black and white points in your image, you can add points or additional curves to refine tonality further.

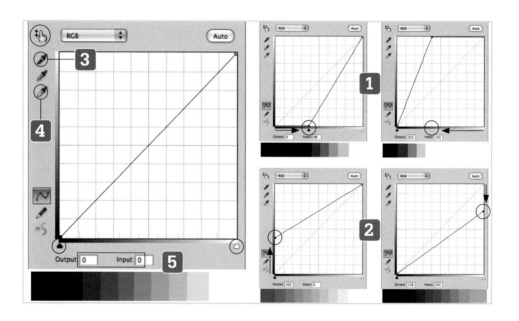

1. To use the sliders, be sure the targeted adjustment mode (the finger icon) is off, and move the sliders along the horizontal axis.

2. To move the black point or white point vertically, click on the end-point in the graph and drag it, or use the up and down arrow keys.

3. Click on the black point dropper and click in the image to force that tone and everything darker to pure black.

4. Click on the white point dropper and click in the image to force that tone and everything lighter to pure white.

5. To dial in specific input and output settings, click on a point and use the Output and Input fields.

 HOT TIP: For a preview of how much of your image is being affected by the horizontal sliders, hold down the Option/Alt key as you drag the slider. Fields of colour will show you what parts of the image are becoming blocked up or blown out as you move the slider.

Adjust colour manually using RGB channels

The colour channels in the Curves adjustment work on the basis of three principles of additive colour:

a) Each channel controls the mixture of a pair of opposing colours that neutralise each other as follows:

- red/cyan
- green/magenta
- blue/yellow

b) Equal amounts of red, green, and blue combine to give a neutral grey, black or white. c) Unequal mixtures of the three spectral primaries produce all other colours.

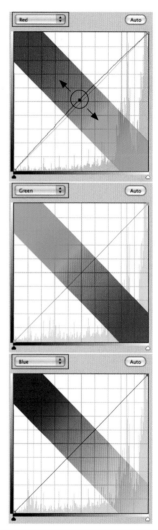

So, if an image looks like it has too much cyan in it, you can compensate by pushing the Red channel curve toward the red. Adding red, green or blue to the curve in Normal mode will lighten the image, and pushing the curve towards cyan, magenta or yellow will darken the image. Because of this, it often makes sense to set the blending mode for colour adjustment curves to colour. In general, you can add a point near the middle of the curve and push up or down in a diagonal direction to apply the adjustment.

1 Add a Curves adjustment layer and rename it to indicate that it's a colour adjustment curve.

2 Set the blending mode of the layer to Colour.

3 Select a channel from the menu immediately above the graph area.

4 Click on the line to add a point and drag to adjust.

5 Work one channel at a time and toggle the adjustment layer on and off with the eyeball icon to evaluate the results.

 HOT TIP: When adjusting images with skin tones, be careful about adding too much green. Skin looks very sickly when it has a greenish cast.

Adjust saturation

Saturation is the relative purity of the colours in an image. There will be times where you will want to increase or decrease the amount of saturation in an image simply for aesthetic reasons. Another reason to reduce saturation is to compensate for the boost in saturation that has occurred when you add a Curves adjustment to an image.

1 Select a layer to define where the Hue/Saturation adjustment will be added.

2 Click on the icon in the Adjustments panel to add a Hue/Saturation layer or select Hue/Saturation from the black and white circle menu at the bottom of the Layers panel.

3 Move the Saturation slider to the left to decrease saturation or to the right to increase.

4 Toggle the adjustment layer on and off with the eyeball icon to evaluate the results.

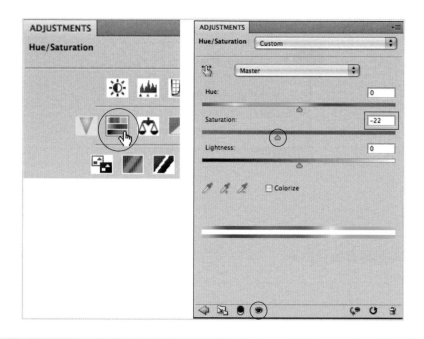

Target a colour and adjust hue and saturation

Using the Hue/Saturation adjustment, you can shift all of the colours in your image, or just some of them. If most of the colours in your photo look good, but that lipstick isn't red enough, targeting the Hues adjustment can do the trick for you.

The two coloured bands at the bottom of the dialogue are a map showing how colours are translated. The top band represents the actual colours in the image, and the bottom band moves to show what each colour translates to. If you don't target a colour, all of the colours in the image will shift. The effect can be quite surreal.

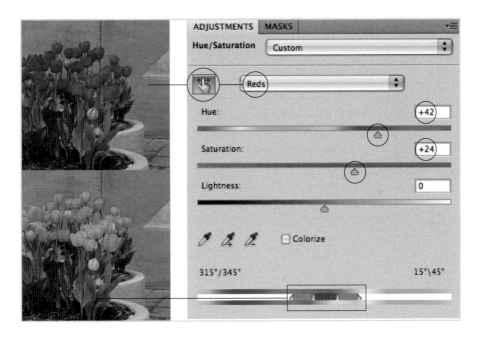

1 Select a layer to determine where your adjustment will be placed and click on the icon in the Adjustments panel to add a Hue/Saturation layer or select Hue/Saturation from the black and white circle menu at the bottom of the Layers panel.

2 Click the finger icon in the upper left corner of the Adjustments panel to activate the targeted adjustment pointer.

3 Press the mouse button down on a colour in the image that you would like to change, and keep holding the button down. The Adjustments panel will update, showing the colours you have targeted.

4 Drag to the right to increase saturation or to the left to decrease saturation, and release the mouse button when you have a satisfactory result.

5 Move the Hue slider to locate a colour that makes the image look more interesting.

6 Readjust the saturation as needed after selecting a new hue.

7 Optional: paint black into the layer mask where you don't want the effect to apply.

 SEE ALSO: Another approach to creating this type of result would be to make a selection using the Color Range command to produce a mask for a Hue/Saturation layer, or even a layer containing colour that is set to a blending mode. See Chapter 8 for details on making selections with Color Range.

Adjust vibrance

The Vibrance adjustment can be thought of as a smart saturation control. It increases or decreases saturation, but protects skin tones, which don't look good when they become oversaturated. It also increases the saturation of highly saturated colours more slowly than it does less saturated colours. Sometimes, a small boost in saturation is still useful, so the Vibrance adjustment layer has a slider for saturation as well, although it is as aggressive as the slider in the Hue/Saturation adjustment.

1 + 100 Saturation in Hue/Saturation.

2 + 100 Saturation in Vibrance.

3 + 100 Vibrance.

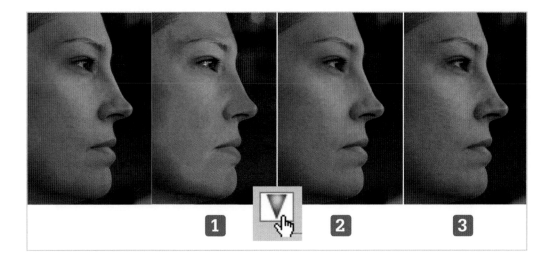

 HOT TIP: A Vibrance setting of -100 still has hints of colour. Low-vibrance images can be an interesting alternative to black and white conversion.

Convert a colour image to black and white

The black and white adjustment layer is an extremely effective and flexible way to transform colour images into rich black and white. It produces a much higher-quality black and white image than turning the saturation all the way down in a Hue/ Saturation adjustment. It works by translating reds, yellows, greens, cyans, blues and magentas into distinct shades of grey that you can adjust.

1 Select a layer to place your Black & White layer above, add the layer, and do any of the following in the panel.

2 Choose a preset from the menu at the top of the panel.

3 Click the finger icon, then drag right or left in the image to lighten or darken the corresponding tones.

4 Adjust the sliders one at a time to find the right tonal mix.

5 Start with the Auto button or a preset, and then tweak, using any of the methods above.

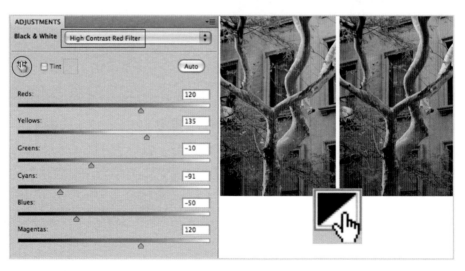

HOT TIP: You can reduce the opacity of a Black & White layer to create an image with a black and white feel, but that has a hint of colour. You can also set a Black & White layer to a blending mode (e.g. Luminosity).

DID YOU KNOW?

A search of the web will turn up dozens of techniques, many of them very complicated, for converting a colour photo to black and white in Photoshop. These were all developed prior to CS3. Most are now obsolete or redundant.

Colourise a black and white image

Adding monochromatic colour back to a black and white image can be a way of giving it a more artistic interpretation. Certain colours (such as sepia) can immediately make a photo look more 'retro', while others can add drama or emotional impact. The Hue/Saturation adjustment has a Colorize option and presets for Sepia and Cyanotype looks, but the preset colours in the Photo Filter offer a broader variety of interesting options. The sequence for creating the image is given below.

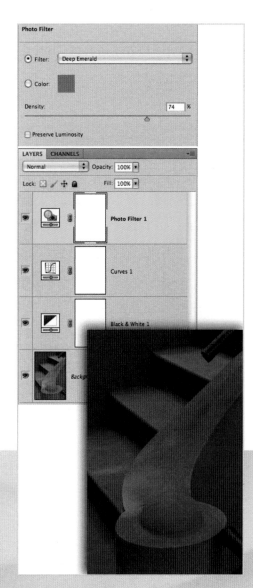

1 Add a Black & White layer, then click Auto to establish the greyscale image.

2 Add a Curves layer to increase brightness and shift the black point slightly to the right.

3 Add a Photo Filter adjustment layer.

4 Select a colour (e.g. Deep Emerald) from the Filter menu or click on the colour chip to select a colour via the colour picker.

5 Adjust density as needed.

6 Be sure to toggle the box marked Preserve Luminosity and evaluate its effect.

7 Optional:
- Add a Curves layer to adjust tones on top of the Photo Filter.
- Tweak colour with Hue/Saturation or Vibrance.
- Experiment with the blending mode of the Photo Filter.

Use a clipping mask

Clipping masks are automatic masks that are defined by the opaque elements of a base layer. The transparent regions of the base layer are rendered transparent in the layers that are clipped to it. This can be very handy in compositing because it allows you to clip colour adjustments to individual bits of your composition so that they match up. You can also clip multiple layers together.

1 Hue/Saturation layer is altering the colours of layers 1 and 2.

2 Option/Alt-click on the dividing line between the adjustment layer and the layer beneath it to clip the adjustment to layer 2.

3 The clipped layer indents and shows a bent arrow icon.

4 Only layer 2 is altered by the Hue/Saturation layer now.

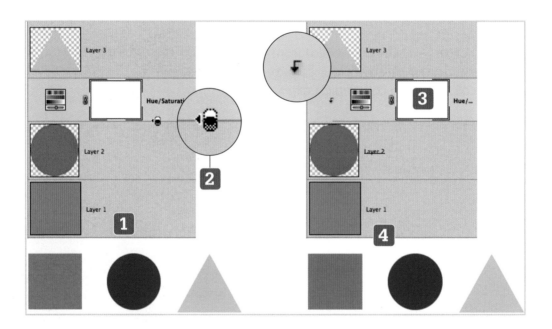

12 Work with text

Introduction

Even if your prime interest in Photoshop is working with images, there are a number of situations where you may want to combine images and text – adding a copyright notice to the bottom of your images or creating a promotional piece, for example. In such cases, you will find Photoshop's Type tools to be very useful.

Use Type tools

The Type tool and the Type Mask tool are grouped under the same button in the Tools panel. Use the Type tool to place type layers containing text in your document. The Type Mask tool doesn't create masks directly; it actually creates a selection that you can use to create a mask. Both tools have horizontal and vertical variations, but you can change the orientation of text with a click in the Options bar as you're typing. Beyond the controls in the Options bar, you can further refine text with the Character and Paragraph panels. Tap T to activate or Shift + T or cycle through the Type tools.

Use the following features in the Options bar:

1. Click the orientation icon to switch between horizontal and vertical text.

2. Set the typeface and style.

3. Set point size and the type of anti-aliasing used.

4. Set alignment.

5. Click the colour chip to set the text colour.

6. Warp the text.

7. Click the icon to open the Character panel (menu bar: Window, Character).

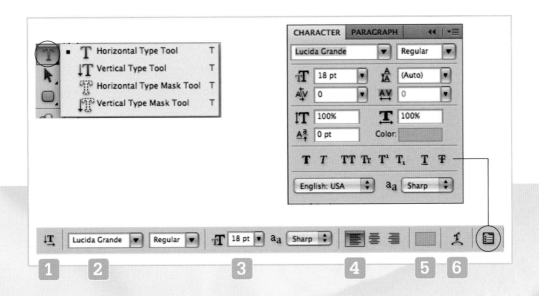

Useful typographic controls in the Character panel:

8 Set leading (line spacing).

9 Use tracking to stretch or shorten individual lines – good for making ragged text look less ragged.

10 Use kerning to manage overlap between character pairs such as V and A.

11 Shift the baseline (useful for text on a path).

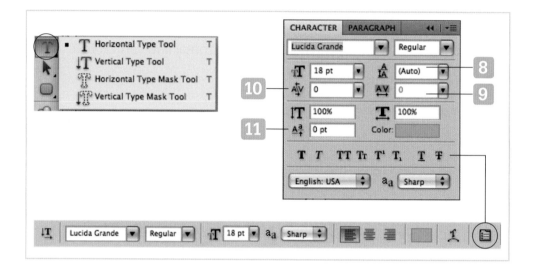

Use the Type tool to make straight-line text

Use this method to add short bits of text to your image. There is a critical bit about editing text on a Mac: when you hit Return, it tells Photoshop that you want to add a new line. When you hit Enter, it tells Photoshop that you have finished editing the text. This is the one place where Return and Enter do not do the same thing.

1 Activate the Type tool. The cursor will change to an I-beam.

2 In the Options panel: check the font, point size and text alignment.

3 Click (do not drag) on the canvas to place an insertion point.

4 Type some text. Notice the blinking cursor.

5 Hit the Enter key, click the tick in the Options bar, or click on a thumbnail in the Layers panel (you can click on the layer's own thumbnail) to commit the text. Hit Esc to cancel.

6 Notice that the new text layer takes its name from its content.

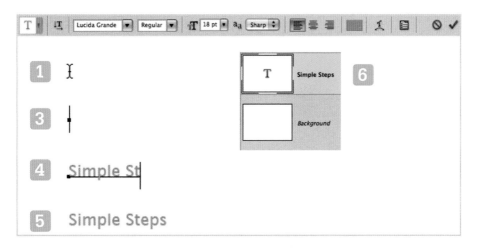

 HOT TIP: While the Type tool is active, you cannot use the letter keys to access other tools in the Tools panel, because the tool sees it all as normal typing. Don't forget to commit the text.

 ALERT: A pitfall of working with the Type tool is that you can click to start some text and then click elsewhere and end up with blank type layers. Just click to select the unwanted layers in the Layers panel and hit the Delete/Backspace key to get rid of them.

Use the Type tool to make wrapping text

To make wrapping text, you define a box that the text fits inside. The size and shape of the box are not critical, since the box can be reshaped later.

1 Activate the Type tool and drag a rectangular shape with the mouse pointer.

2 Type text into the box. When it hits the edge, you will see it wrap.

3 Use the handles on the text box to reshape it.

4 Notice that the text reflows to fit the box, and that it is clipped when the box is too small.

5 Hit the Enter key, click the tick in the Options bar, or click a thumbnail in the layers panel to commit your edits.

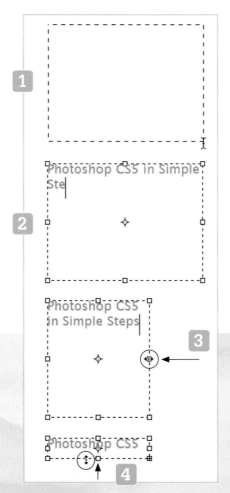

Edit committed text and reshape wrapping text

If you have committed a Type layer, you can edit it at any time. If the text is wrapping text, you can reshape the box when you reopen the text for editing.

Method A:

1. Double-click on the thumbnail of the Type layer that you want to edit. The Type tool will automatically activate and the text box will open with all of its text selected.

2. For wrapping text: drag the resizing handles to change the shape of the text box.

3. Select and edit text as in any standard text editor.

4. Hit Enter when you are satisfied.

5. Notice that the layer name has been updated.

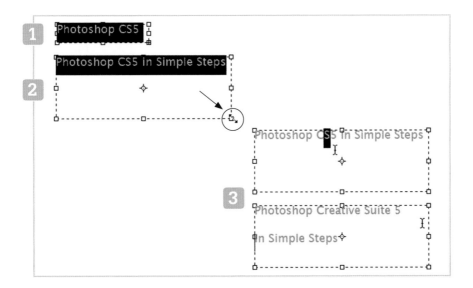

Method B:

6 Select the Type tool from the Tools panel.

7 Drag the cursor over the text that you want to edit. The text will become selected and the text box will open for editing.

8 Note: if you overshoot the text box, a new text box will be created – hit Esc or delete the unwanted Type layer.

9 Edit the text as desired and hit Enter when you are satisfied.

 HOT TIP: When editing text, you can double-click to select a word or triple-click to select an entire line.

! **ALERT:** On the Mac, the Return and Enter keys usually do the same thing, but each has a distinct function when editing text. Hitting Return adds a new line to the text, while Enter commits the text entry.

Alter text with the Options and Character panels

The Options bar and the Character panel offer additional ways of editing the contents of any Type layer. Some editing options are listed below.

1 Begin editing the text by using any of the methods described in the previous section.

2 Select text by doing any of the following:

- Select all of the text using Command/Ctrl + A.
- Double-click to select a word.
- Triple-click to select a line.
- Drag across text to select.
- Click to place the cursor, then Shift-click at another point in the text to select all text in between.

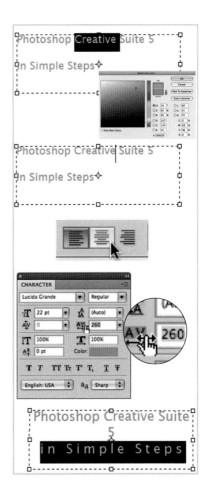

3 To change text colour: select the text you wish to change and click on the colour chip in the Options bar to select a colour via the colour picker.

4 To change point size: select text and then use the size control in either the Options bar or the Character panel.

5 To show the Character panel, either click on the Character panel button in the Options bar or select Window, Character from the menu bar.

6 Select all or part of a single line of text and adjust the Tracking in the Character panel to see how it affects the spacing between letters, shortening and lengthening the line.

7 Other controls in the Character panel to experiment with: Leading, Horizontal scale and Vertical scale.

 HOT TIP: Savvy typographers will vary the tracking of text line-by-line to make good-looking justified text. It often works much better than setting the alignment of the text to fully justified.

Transform text

Photoshop has several transformation modes that work with live text. The advantage is that the text can be edited even after you have transformed it, and the transformation can also be readjusted.

1 Click on a Type layer to select it, then hit Command/Ctrl + T to enter Free Transform.

2 Drag the handles to transform as you would any other layer:

- Shift-drag the corner handles to scale, Option/Alt + Shift-drag to scale from the centre.
- Control-click/right-click for a menu of additional transformation modes.

3 To begin warping the text, click the Warp modes button in the Options bar.

4 Choose a warp style from the menu and adjust the settings.

5 Hit Return/Enter or click the tick icon in the Options bar to commit the changes.

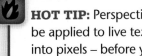 **HOT TIP:** Perspective is one transformation mode that cannot be applied to live text. You can rasterise the text – turning it into pixels – before you transform it, but the text will no longer be editable. If you convert the text to a Smart Object, though, you can apply the perspective transformation and still edit the contents of the Smart Object if you need to.

Clip an image to text

In the previous chapter, a clipping mask was used to attach an adjustment to a single layer. In this example, we'll look at a different application of the same principle: stylised text will serve as the base layer to mask an image.

1 Edit your text. For this feature to work well, you want your text to provide a good amount of surface for the image to show through. Thick, bold, slab-type fonts like Rockwell, Egyptian and Soho Gothic are very useful.

2 Position your image layer directly above your text layer.

3 Hover the mouse pointer over the dividing line between the two layers and hold down the Option/Alt key. The icon will change to indicate that the layers are about to be clipped together. Click to clip the layers.

4 Use the Move tool to drag the image layer so that interesting or salient bits show through the text.

5 In this case, the imagery looked weak against the solid white background: click the layer and use Command/Ctrl + I to invert to black.

13 Resize and resample

Introduction

This brief chapter is about image size and quality. Whenever you deal with making your image appear larger or smaller, you'll have to look at the question of resizing versus resampling. If you're printing, you may be able to simply resize your file. If you're saving for the web or making a large exhibition print, then you're likely to resample.

Resizing is a non-destructive way of making larger or smaller prints. When you resize your image, you don't alter the pixels in your file, you tell the printer to make larger or smaller dots. The size of the dots determines the size (and quality) of the prints.

When you resample an image for the web, only the pixel dimensions are relevant. Unlike a printer, the resolution of the viewer's screen is fixed. In a web browser, a 300 × 500 – pixel image at 72 dpi will look the same as a 300 × 500 pixel image at 300 dpi, even though the 72 dpi image would print four times larger than the 300 dpi image.

When you resample an image, Photoshop literally takes your image apart and rebuilds it. Increasing the file dimensions is called up-sampling, and it works by spreading the pixels in your file apart to span the new size, and synthesising new pixels to fill in the gaps. When you down-sample your image, Photoshop calculates new pixels based on how much the original pixels would have overlapped. The result is that data are discarded. Use Save As ... when you save a resampled file. You never want to replace your original with a resampled version because even the best resampling calculations degrade your image somewhat.

Resize for printing

With a 10-megapixel camera, you can print up to about 27 cm by 41 cm without having to resample. In the example shown here, reducing the resolution to 240 ppi increased the width of the image by more than 6 centimetres. Chances are, there is no detectable difference in quality.

1 Choose Image, Image Size ... from the menu bar. The Image Size dialogue will appear.

2 Make sure the box marked Resample Image near the bottom of the dialogue is not ticked.

3 Enter a width or a height that best fits the paper you will be printing on.

4 Note the resolution. If the number falls well below 240 pixels/inch, you should consider resampling.

5 Click OK.

6 If you plan to print regularly at this size, save your file, and these dimensions will be stored in the file.

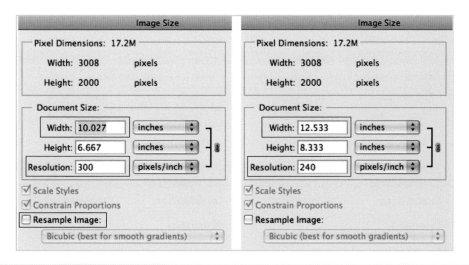

? DID YOU KNOW?

240 dpi is a good resolution to target because it's a good fit with the resolution of most inkjet printers. Low resolution means bigger dots. Once the dots get to somewhere around 150 dpi, they become visible at arm's length. That's when it's time to consider resampling to increase the ppi in the image. We use ppi to describe the pixels/inch on a screen and dpi to describe the dots/inch in a printer, so the two terms are analogous.

Resample using Image Size

The Image Size dialogue is the main tool for changing the size of files, whether you are resampling or not. Fit Image, a simpler tool for down-sampling images, will be covered later in this chapter.

1 Select Image, Image Size ... from the menu bar to open the dialogue.

2 Make sure that the boxes labelled Resample Image and Constrain Proportions are ticked.

3 For the web, enter a width or height in pixels. The other dimension will be calculated for you.

4 When you are making the image smaller, use either Bicubic Sharper or Bicubic.

5 For printing, you may not need to resample. Check the resolution first: untick the Resample Image box and enter the dimensions you want to print.

6 If the resolution goes well below 240 dpi, tick the Resample Image box and enter the resolution you wish to use (240 ppi is a good resolution to use for most ink-jet printers).

7 If you are making the image larger, use either Bicubic Smoother or Bicubic.

8 Click OK when you have established dimensions and resolution.

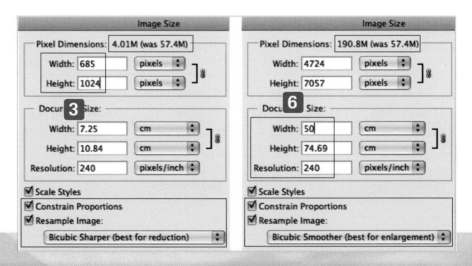

HOT TIP: In printing, there are three magic dpi values to aim for. These values are the easiest resolutions for your printer software to work with. If you are printing to an ink-jet or giclée printer, 240 dpi prints very well, and 360 dpi is theoretically better, though you will be hard-pressed to tell the difference. Laser printers and digital C printers typically work best with 300 dpi output.

Use the 110 per cent resample solution for big enlargements

If you need to make your file a lot larger, you might get better results scaling it up step-wise, rather than doing it in one jump with Bicubic Smoother. The idea is that resampling in small increments makes any sampling errors less obvious.

1 Select Image, Image Size ... from the menu bar.

2 Tick Constrain Proportions, and Resample Image.

3 Choose Bicubic.

4 Enter 110 per cent into one of the Pixel Dimensions fields.

5 Check the width and height fields: they will display the resulting dimensions.

6 Click OK to make a resample pass.

7 Repeat steps 4–6 until the document size reaches your target size. On your last pass, if 110 per cent produces a size that is over your target size, enter the target size into the Document Size Width or Height field.

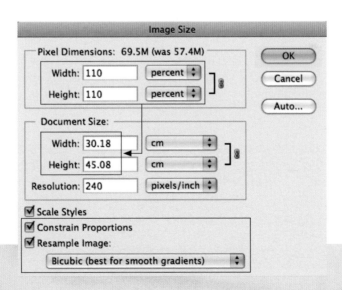

? DID YOU KNOW?

Photoshop can record Actions to help automate processes like step-wise resampling.

Resample using Fit Image

Fit Image is a useful utility in Photoshop, which allows you to specify the dimensions of a box that your images need to fit inside. That way, it can work with either horizontally or vertically oriented images. Photoshop will then calculate how to resample the images for you.

1 Select File, Automate, Fit Image ... from the menu bar. The Fit Image dialogue will appear.

2 Enter the target Width and Height dimensions in pixels.

3 Click OK.

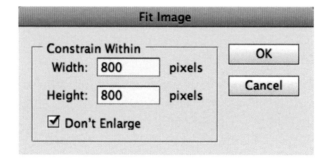

ALERT: As is the case with Image Size, resampling is a destructive edit, so be sure to use Save As ...

14 Sharpen

Introduction

Certain images will benefit from some amount of sharpening; the effect can give additional snap to details. However, it is optional and a matter of taste. Sharpening in Photoshop is really a misnomer. It cannot make an out-of-focus image look focused. What it can do is emphasise the edges of things, which gives the impression of sharpness.

Beyond personal taste, the amount of sharpening to be applied depends on what you plan to do with the image. You will probably find that more sharpening is required for prints than for posting the same image on the web.

Before you sharpen your image, it is a good idea to resize or resample it as needed, and zoom in so that you are seeing at least part of the image at approximately the physical output size. For information on resampling and resizing, see the steps outlined in Chapter 13.

Use Zoom to view at output size

It's important to evaluate your sharpening at a size that closely approximates the output, otherwise you'll probably add too much or too little. Here, we'll make a shape of a known size, and use the Zoom tool to set the proper screen magnification.

1 Activate the rectangular Marquee tool and drag out a shape on the screen. The size and shape aren't critical. A box of 'marching ants' will appear.

2 Choose Select, Transform Selection from the menu bar.

3 In the Options bar, enter a round number into the Width box (e.g. 10 cm). Hit Return/Enter twice: first to set the field and secondly to commit the transform.

4 You now have a size sample on-screen.

5 Mark off the width you defined in step 3 on a piece of paper.

6 Hold the paper up to the screen and set the zoom percentage so that the marching ant selection on screen matches up with your reference marks.

7 Use Command/Ctrl + D to deselect.

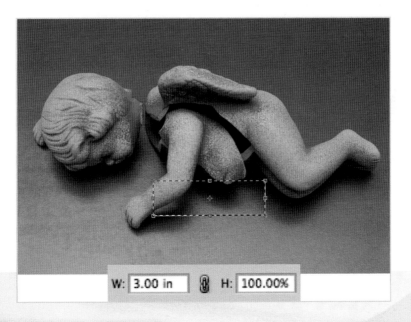

W: 3.00 in   H: 100.00%

 HOT TIP: Once you determine the magnification percentage, write it down so that you can just type it in when needed.

Use Smart Sharpen

The biggest problem with sharpening is that many people overdo it. The technique outlined below makes it easy to apply sharpening effectively.

1 Begin by stamping a layer at the top of your layer stack to apply sharpening to (see Chapter 5). Click on the layer to select it.

2 Use the Zoom technique outlined earlier in this chapter to view your image at output size.

3 Hit the Tab key to hide the panels temporarily and use the Hand tool, Bird's Eye View, etc. to show an area that you want to sharpen, like the eyes, hair or something with important texture.

4 From the menu bar, select Filter, Sharpen, Smart Sharpen … The Smart Sharpen dialogue box will appear. Position the dialogue so that you can see your image and the dialogue controls.

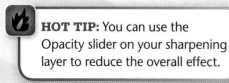

HOT TIP: You can use the Opacity slider on your sharpening layer to reduce the overall effect.

5 In the dialogue, make sure the Remove option is set to Lens Blur, and leave More Accurate unticked.

6 Move the Amount slider all the way to the right, so that the amount reads 500 per cent. Your image may look pretty bad at this point; that's fine.

7 Move the Radius slider all the way to the left – 0.1 pixels.

8 Now, slowly increase the radius by sliding it a small amount at a time to the right until your image begins to look brittle. This is your sharpening radius.

9 Move the Amount slider to the left until the brittle quality just disappears.

10 Click to toggle the Preview box a few times, toggling the effect to evaluate how the sharpening is working. Readjust as needed.

11 Click the OK button to apply the effect, and hit the Tab key to restore the panels.

ALERT: Be careful about sharpening skin. It brings out pores and texture. You can use a layer mask to hide the sharpening on skin – use the Color Range command to assist in selecting the skin as you create the mask.

Sharpen with the High Pass filter

High-pass sharpening produces a slightly different look and is particularly good for emphasising the shine in surfaces like jewellery. Use either style of sharpening, or none at all, as your image requires.

1. Begin by stamping a layer at the top of your layer stack to apply sharpening to (see Chapter 5). Click on the layer to select it.

2. Use the Zoom feature to view your image at output size, using the steps outlined earlier in this chapter.

3. Select Filter, Other, High Pass ... from the menu bar. The High Pass dialogue box will appear.

4. Move the Radius slider in small increments and notice when the features you want to sharpen appear as faint lines. You can increase the radius slightly from that point, but eventually you will get an unsightly halo. In most cases, you will find that a radius between 3 and 10 pixels works best.

5. Click the OK button.

6. Choose Image, Adjustments, Desaturate from the menu bar. This eliminates any potential colour fringing that can come from the High Pass effect.

7. Change the blending mode of the layer to Overlay.

Possible ways to refine the effect further:

- Reduce the opacity of the layer.
- Use Soft Light blending mode instead of Overlay.
- Increase the effect by duplicating the layer.
- Select the sharpening layer and Option/Alt-click on the Add Layer Mask icon to add a black mask. The sharpening will disappear from the entire image. Paint with white to restore the effect to specific areas. Use a soft brush at reduced Opacity/Flow for a controlled, gradual build-up.

15 Print

Introduction

Photoshop's forte in printing is colour management, but Photoshop directly controls only half of the printing process; the printer driver controls the rest. With the release of CS5, Photoshop now embeds the print settings in the documents you print. This can be a time-saver, and it also brings about a small change in the printing workflow from earlier versions.

The examples in this chapter feature the drivers from the popular Epson 2880 printer. Because printer drivers can look very different by make, model and operating system, your printer driver's screens may look different, but the principles and often the language used will be exactly the same.

Prepare for printing

When you are ready to print, your first concern is setting the proper print size and resolution. Depending upon your needs, you may either resize or resample the image (see Chapter 13). After that, the question of sharpening arises. Whether or not to sharpen is a matter of personal preference, and the best time to apply sharpening, if at all, is after the print resolution is set.

The next consideration is the colour profile and bit depth you wish to work with. If you let Photoshop manage the colours, you can print from wide-gamut colour spaces like Adobe RGB and Prophoto RGB (which absolutely requires 16-bit printing), but if you let the printer manage the colours, most will only give good results with a file that has been converted to sRGB.

When Photoshop prints, it converts the colours in the image to the colour space of the ink and paper combination of the printer. Epson, Canon and many paper manufacturers all provide printer profiles on the web. There are also companies that make custom profiles, and a number of tools are available to create profiles specific to your printer and the paper you use with it.

For the most accurate colour matching between your screen and printer, it's best to work with a wide-gamut display that has also been profiled. X-Rite's ColorMunki is a simple and effective tool for profiling both displays and printers. If the brightness of your screen is set very high, you will consistently find that your prints come out dark. Turning the brightness down may make your work look less dazzling on screen, but you'll get better print matching.

When you print, you actually interact with two distinct pieces of software: Photoshop and the printer's driver. Manufacturers often update their printer drivers, especially after Microsoft and Apple release new system software. Check the manufacturer's website periodically for updates.

Printing often goes faster when you print from a flattened file. You can flatten the file before printing (menu: Layer, Flatten Image), and then undo the flattening or close the flattened file without saving it, when you're finished.

 HOT TIP: To use colour profiles, you store them in a particular folder on your computer. If you are working on Mac OS X, you store them either in /Library/ColorSync/Profiles, or /Users/<username>/Library/ColorSync/Profiles. If you are on Windows XP or Vista, place them in \Windows\system32\spool\drivers\color.

Print with Photoshop colour management

When Photoshop manages colours, it translates the colours in your image into the colour space of the printer profile. With an accurate printer profile, Photoshop can produce highly accurate colour prints.

This page presents a summary of the entire process. The rest of this chapter will discuss these topics in greater detail.

1 Select File, Print ... from the menu bar: the Print dialogue will appear.

2 Select the printer.

3 Send 16-bit data when available.

4 Edit and save print settings: this uses your printer driver's dialogue.

5 Set page layout parameters.

6 Set colour management parameters.

7 Check to see that your paper is properly loaded.

8 Click Print.

Edit and save print settings

Photoshop stores the specified printer in the document along with its print settings. Click the Print Settings button to open the printer driver dialogue. Because Photoshop and the printer driver have limited communication, you have to set the printer and 16-bit printing in two places, Photoshop cannot turn off the driver's colour management, and the printer driver cannot select the appropriate colour profile for you.

Your printer driver may have a different interface than the one shown here. Check with your printer manufacturer for additional information on using its driver.

1 Choose your printer from the menu.

2 When available, tick Send 16-bit Data.

3 Use the orientation buttons to rotate the image.

4 Click Print Settings ... to open the print driver dialogue.

In the Epson print dialogue:

5 Select your printer and paper size from the menus. The paper size selection also determines which path to load the paper through: Use the Manual – Roll size options to feed stiffer paper and rolls through the alternate slot.

6 Select Print Settings from the menu in the middle of the dialogue. (If you don't see the menu, click the button with the triangle to expand the dialogue.)

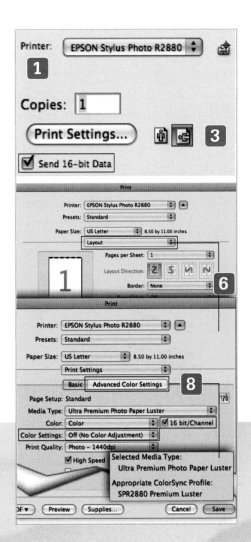

7 Set the media type to match the kind of paper you are using. (If you are not sure which media type is best to use, check with your paper's manufacturer.)

8 Click Advanced Color Settings for advice on which profile to use for colour management and then click Basic to return to the main screen.

9 Select Color and tick 16 bit/Channel if you are printing from a 16-bit file.

10 Important: set Color Settings to Off (No Color Adjustment) because Photoshop is managing the colour. If your print comes out with a strong magenta cast, it's probably because you didn't turn this setting off.

11 Choose a Print Quality setting. Photo – 1440 dpi works best for most situations. (You will be hard-pressed to see a difference with SuperPhoto, though it uses more ink.)

12 Optional: tick High Speed for faster bi-directional printing.

13 Click Save to store your settings in the document.

> **!** **ALERT:** If you see fine horizontal lines in the print, try turning off the High Speed setting and reprinting. Some papers require special paper feed, and some require adjusting the platen gap. See your printer documentation for more details.

Set page layout parameters

Use the page layout parameters to position the image precisely on the page.

1 Use the menu at the top of the dialogue to select your printer.

2 Enter the number of copies.

3 If your image is turned incorrectly, use the rotation buttons to reorient it.

4 To move your image off-centre, untick Center Image. Click in the fields and type values, or use the arrow keys to move the image on the page.

5 You can tick Scale to Fit Media to shrink your image if you have not resized or resampled prior to printing.

6 To scale or position your image visually: put a tick mark next to Bounding Box to show handles. Drag the edges or the corners of the box to scale the image. Drag inside the box to reposition on the page.

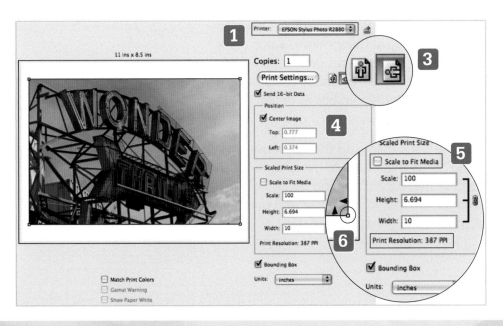

ALERT: If you use scaling, watch out for print resolutions that are substantially less than 240 ppi. Take note of the indicated print resolution and use that to resize later.

Set colour management parameters

The colour management parameters are essential for getting quality colour out of your printer.

1 Make sure that the circle next to Document is filled in.

2 Select Photoshop Manages Colors from the Color Handling menu. The alert reminding you to disable the printer's colour management refers to step 11 in the 'Edit and save print settings' section earlier in this chapter.

3 In the Printer Profile menu, select a profile that matches your printer and paper combination. You can use the profile recommended by the Epson driver.

4 Choose either Relative Colorimetric or Perceptual for the Rendering Intent. Even though Perceptual can shift colours in your image more, colour gradients are less likely to break down. Relative Colorimetric is not recommended if you are printing a Prophoto RGB document – it will probably cause gradients to posterise into bands of flat colour.

5 If you have been following the workflow outlined at the beginning of this chapter, this is the final step before sending the job off to the printer. Review your settings and press Print to start the print job.

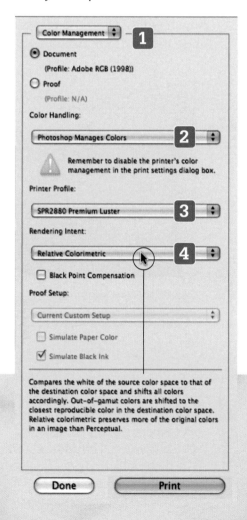

 HOT TIP: When you hover the mouse pointer over the items in the Color Management section, a description of their function appears in the box at the bottom of the dialogue.

Print in black and white

Printing in black and white is very similar to printing in colour and works the same, whether you are printing a greyscale document or a converted colour image containing a Black and White adjustment layer. Of course with a Black and White layer, you can print black and white and colour versions of the image from the same file.

When printing in black and white, the difference in the process comes down to the settings you use in the printer driver. This example shows the printer driver of the Epson R2880 printer; however, there are other printers that have similar features and capabilities.

The first part of this chapter discussed how to establish the page layout and colour management settings in detail. That process is the same for black and white. The print settings are established as follows:

1 Click Print Settings ... to open the driver dialogue.

2 Select Print Settings from the menu in the middle of the dialogue.

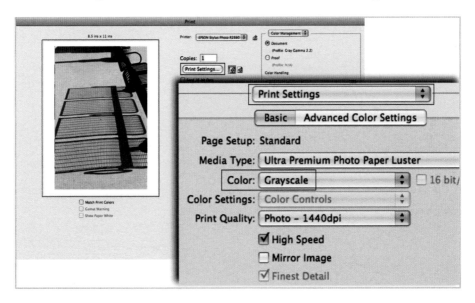

3 Select the appropriate media type.

4 Choose Grayscale from the Color menu.

5 Set the Print Quality (e.g. Photo – 1140 dpi).

6 Optional: tick High Speed.

7 Click Save.

 HOT TIP: Epson's print drivers have two black and white modes: Grayscale, and Advanced Black and White mode. The Advanced mode provides a way of colour-toning your black and white images; however, it is better to do such toning in Photoshop where you have more control and more options.

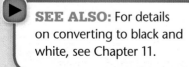 **SEE ALSO:** For details on converting to black and white, see Chapter 11.

Top 10 Photoshop CS5 Problems Solved

My keyboard shortcuts aren't working or Photoshop just beeps

When the text is highlighted or a blinking cursor appears inside a value box (e.g. a size field in the Options bar), that field is said to have 'focus'. This can sometimes interfere with keyboard shortcuts, because the field soaks up the keystroke. Sometimes, your typing may appear in the field, but at other times Photoshop will just beep. Hit Return/ Enter to commit changes to the field and take the focus off the field. In some cases, you may need to reset the value of the field before you can commit it.

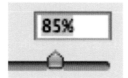

My cursor suddenly looks like a simple crosshair

If you're seeing a cursor that looks like a dot surrounded by four radiating lines, you could be in Precise Cursor mode, or perhaps you tapped the M key and activated the Marquee tool.

1 Turn off Caps Lock to exit Precise Cursor mode.

2 The Marquee tool cursor is similar. Check the Tools panel to be sure the right tool is selected.

3 If neither of these is the case, your brush size is probably very small: tap the] (right square bracket) key repeatedly to make your brush larger. (Make sure you didn't turn Caps Lock on while trying step 1.)

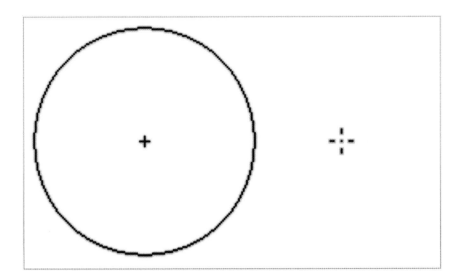

I keep losing my Marquee tool cursor

The mouse pointer for the Marquee tool is very small and fine (and so are other precise cursors), so it's easy to have it 'submarine' and lose track of it. Press the space bar to convert your current tool temporarily to the Hand tool. If you still don't see it, wiggle the mouse a little. You should see the cursor waving back at you. Reposition the cursor where you want it, and then release the space bar.

All my tools and panels have just disappeared

When you hit the Tab key in Photoshop, the panels are hidden away. In Bridge, the right and left columns are hidden. This almost undocumented feature can actually be very handy. It's just scary when you don't know about it.

Hit the Tab key again to restore.

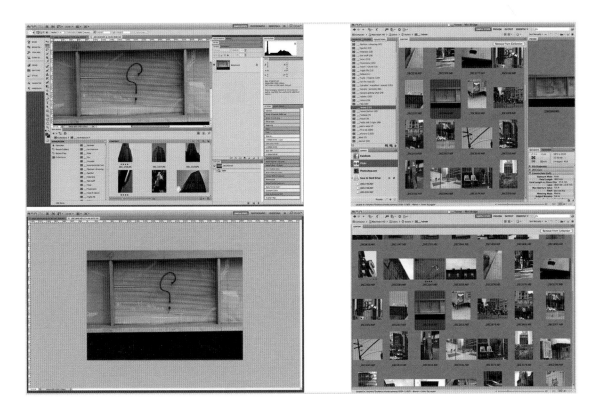

I can't see any painting

When your painting is not showing up, there are several possibilities (this is not a comprehensive list):

1 There is an active selection, and you are attempting to paint outside the selection. Choose Select, Deselect from the menu to release the selection and try again.

2 Your edits are being applied to the wrong layer. An opaque layer is covering the active layer that is receiving your edits. You may have to step back in the History panel to undo the changes you made, then select the intended layer and try again.

3 The active layer is inside a group that has its visibility switched off. Turn the visibility of the group back on to see your edits.

4 Your layer has a mask on it that is at least partially blacked out.

5 You might be in Quick Mask mode and painting with a white brush. More on this on page 287.

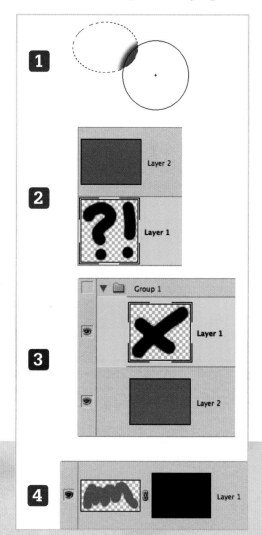

I'm getting a message about a missing colour profile

If you open a file without a colour profile, the colours you see may be completely wrong. To address the problem, Photoshop displays the Missing Profile dialogue so that you can assign a colour profile. If you pick the wrong colour profile, your colours will still be wrong, but as long as you don't also convert the document to the working space, that's not a problem, because you can assign a different profile after you open it. This example assumes the working colour space is Adobe RGB. (See Chapter 1 for more details.)

1 If you know the file was created in the Adobe RGB space, click the circle next to Assign working RGB: to do so.

2 If the file came from the web, it's a good guess that it is an sRGB image. Click the circle next to Assign profile: to select it and choose sRGB from the profile menu.

3 If you are not certain about the right colour profile, do not tick the box to convert to working RGB. If you plan to convert to another colour space after you have finished editing, it is also not a good idea to convert to the working space. Converting can shift colours and degrade your image.

4 Click OK to open the image. If the colours look wrong, choose Edit, Assign Profile ... from the menu bar. In the Assign Profile dialogue, leave Preview ticked, and click back and forth between Working RGB and Profile to see how the colours in your image change. Use the profile menu to compare results among Adobe RGB, sRGB and ProPhoto RGB. Click OK when you have found the best result.

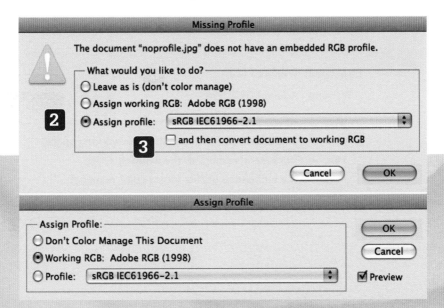

I'm getting a message about an embedded profile mismatch

If you set the appropriate option in your colour settings, whenever you open a file that has an embedded colour profile that does not match the working colour space, you will see the Embedded Profile Mismatch dialogue. For example, with the working space set to Adobe RGB, when you open an sRGB or ProPhoto RGB image, you will see the dialogue.

The choice you're being asked to make is whether you want to work in the colour space that the image defines, or whether you want to convert the colours to the working space. Using the embedded profile is generally the best approach, especially if you plan to convert to another colour space after you have finished editing, since each time you convert colours, there is a chance you will get colour shifts.

If you choose to convert the colours, there is less of a downside when you convert to a larger colour space (i.e. from sRGB to Adobe RGB or from Adobe RGB to ProPhoto RGB). Converting to a smaller colour space is more likely to degrade your image. The most problematic conversion would be to go from ProPhoto RGB to sRGB.

If your image is in sRGB and you plan to adjust colours and tones, and simply use the file for printing, there is some benefit to upgrading the colour space to Adobe RGB. If you are opening a web file to adjust it and then post it back on the web, there is no reason to convert from sRGB to Adobe RGB and back to sRGB.

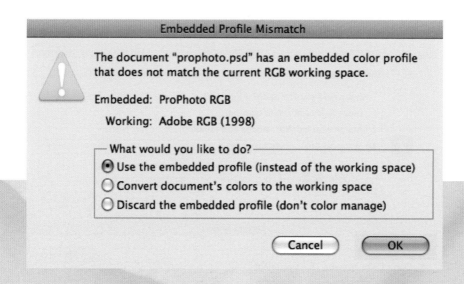

My layers have gone out of alignment

Chances are, you accidentally pressed the Command/Ctrl key in the midst of using another tool (e.g. the Brush tool). Most tools, including the Lasso, Marquee, Healing Brush and Brush tool, temporarily convert to the Move tool when you press the Command/Ctrl key.

Hold the Command/Ctrl key down and notice the shape of the cursor. Keep an eye out for that shape.

If you look at your History panel, you will probably see the Move state nestled in the middle of your other activities. To fix the problem, you can click on the History state directly above the Move and continue forward from there.

My prints are coming out very magenta

The culprit is likely to be double colour management. Check your printer's colour management control. When Photoshop is managing colours, the colour settings should be turned off in the printer. The illustration here shows the reminder messsage in Photoshop's Print dialogue and the Print Settings section of the driver dialogue for the Epson R2880 on Mac OS X. Driver dialogues will vary by make, model and operating system.

1 Warning message in the colour management section of Photoshop's print dialogue.

2 Double-management.

3 Correct setting.

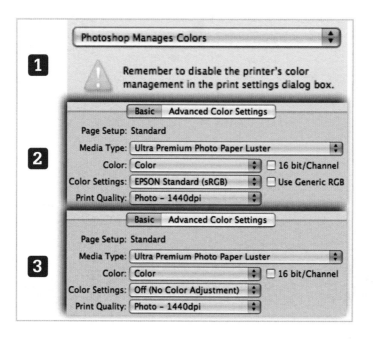

SEE ALSO: See Chapter 15 for details on printing with colour management.

I've fallen into Quick Mask (and don't know it)

If you're in Quick Mask mode and you have the foreground colour set to white, it will seem as if the Brush tool is not working. If the foreground colour is set to black the Brush tool will seem to be laying down colour, but not black. If you're not expecting this, it can be very disorienting.

Photoshop does give some hints that you are in Quick Mask mode, but they're relatively subtle. First, the Quick Mask button in the Tools panel darkens. Second, the active layer will be highlighted in grey. Third, the document title will actually say Quick Mask. Fourth, the foreground and background colours will switch to black and white.

To exit Quick Mask mode, tap the Q key.

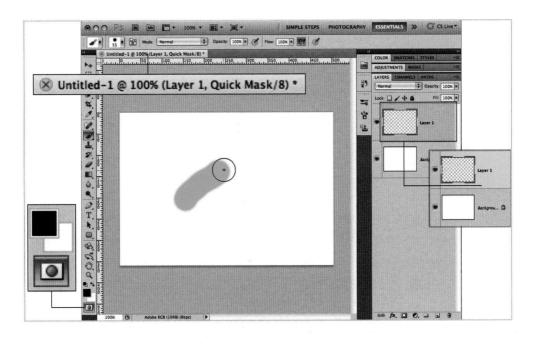